Hounds and Terriers

Hounds and Terriers

Ronald Delaney

BLANDFORD PRESS
POOLE · DORSET

First published in the U.K. 1984 by Blandford Press, Link House, West Street, Poole, Dorset BH15 1LL.

Copyright © 1984 Blandford Press Ltd.

Distributed in the United States by Sterling Publishing Co., Inc., 2 Park Avenue, New York, N.Y. 10016.

British Library Cataloguing in Publication Data

Delaney, Ronald
  Hounds and terriers.
  1. Hounds 2. Terriers
  I. Title
  636.7'73   SF426.H6

  ISBN 0-7137-1371-2

Typeset by Megaron Typesetting, Bournemouth.

Printed and bound in U.K. by Biddles Ltd., Guildford.

Contents

Author's Preface

To choose the best of the terriers, nothing could be more difficult . . . or more fascinating. The matadors of the group, the Bull Terriers, White, Coloured, Standard and Miniature, and the Staffords, all have the necessary qualities of strength, stamina and courage in full measure. Of the short-legged terriers, the underground workers, the Glen of Imaal is without doubt the most formidable. For those who appreciate beautiful line and superb movement, the Airedale, with its fine outline and elegant gait, is clearly supreme. If one looks for a dog to run with the hounds, the Border Terrier has few equals, especially in the rocky hill country like the Scottish border where it originates. Indeed, the hounds present the same problem as the terriers: which of them would best suit your own home, family circle, temperament and way of life? Perhaps it would be the aristocratic Afghan, the cheerful Beagle, the clean-footed Whippet or the merry little Dachs. It all depends therefore on personal taste, and on the job the dog is intended to perform, when a final choice is made.

Before making that choice it is essential to know the indispensable facts about each breed and to this end are given the origin, history, characteristics and statistics of all the twenty-four breeds classified in the Kennel Club's Terrier group and of the twenty-six in the Hound group, together with sections on the Jack Russell Terrier, the Welsh Foxhound, the American Foxhound and the Lurcher. Photographs of present-day show winners and others illustrate each breed. Detailed descriptions are based on the standards of the Kennel Club to which my grateful acknowledgements are expressed, and thanks are also due to Marc Henrie, David Dalton, Frank Garwood, Anne Roslin-Williams, Lionel Young, Infocus, High Society Studios and the American Kennel Club for their excellent photographic contributions. The comprehensive bibliography will be of special interest to the student of natural history and I would like to express my gratitude to Mr. John Fisher, F.L.A., of the Guildhall Library, London, for his invaluable help in tracing rare books. My thanks also to Maggie O'Hanlon of Blandford Press for her help in preparing this book for publication.

Ronald Delaney
Cerne Abbas 1984

Introduction

The earliest concrete evidence of the existence of dogs being used by Man in the chase of game is pictorial. The ancient Eastern Greyhound, a type which has hardly changed in appearance over thousands of years, is clearly depicted in Egyptian friezes and mural paintings in the tombs of the Pharaohs, in the colourful mosaics illustrating hunting scenes in the Bardo Museum of Tunis and on Grecian frescoes in the Mycenaean Palace of Tiryns. Dogs resembling the Afghan, the Saluki and the Sloughi can easily be recognised there, as can the prick-eared types, such as the Pharaoh Hound, the Ibizan Hound and the Basenji. It is certain that the sighthound group of canines is the oldest of the hounds and that the scenthounds did not evolve until much later.

The sighthounds, or running dogs, of the East, the silent hunters, although generally similar to each other in appearance and use, do have certain distinguishing features, depending largely on their place of origin and the terrain they are accustomed to work. For instance, the Borzoi and Afghan from the northern regions have a profuse coat to protect them from the intense cold, whilst the Borzoi from Central and Southern Russia — the Tchistopsovaya — and the Saluki and the Sloughi are much shorter-haired, albeit with a certain amount of feathering in the case of the Tchistopsovaya and the Saluki. The hounds with erect ears from warmer climates — the Basenji, the Pharaoh Hound, the Ibizan Hound and the Portuguese Podengo — all have short, sleek coats.

The methods of hunting and the game hunted vary considerably. The Afghans and Salukis were trained to work with falcons, which mounted huntsmen carried on their fists until the quarry was sighted, whether wolf, gazelle or antelope. The bird would then be released and the dogs would follow it with their eyes; suddenly it would swoop onto the head of its prey and hold on until the dogs were able to catch up and drag it to the ground. Great speed is necessary for such sport and the Afghan and Saluki are well endowed in this respect. The Borzoi was used in a similar way by the Russian Imperial Court especially to hunt wolf, hence its former name of Russian Wolfhound. The Sloughi, however, was used by mounted North African tribesmen to hunt gazelle and jackal in the Sahara, but without the help of hawks. The Irish Wolfhound, the Scottish Deerhound, the Greyhound and the Whippet all belong to this family of sighthounds.

The prick-eared hounds — the Basenji, the Pharaoh, the Ibizan and the Podengo — hunt in still different ways. The Basenji is a pack-hunter, its main work being to locate in silence and drive small game into nets stretched between trees. The Pharaoh, the Ibizan and the Podengo are used for coursing hare and rabbit, as well as in the rôle of scenthound in the chase of deer and occasionally bear.

The scenthounds proper did not make their appearance until later and it was largely in the western world, and in France in particular, that hunting with this type of hound in packs was first brought to perfection. The Elkhound, a comparative newcomer to this section and of which there are several varieties, is of the Spitz type and is used for hunting the large deer in Norwegian forests; its job is to chase and harass its quarry in similar fashion to the Rhodesian Ridgeback when hunting lion. The distinctive features of the scenthounds are their acute powers of smell, some like the Bloodhound being able to track down a quarry from an old scent, and the magic sound of their baying as they move off in full cry. They are also more heavily built and slower moving than the sighthounds and they have more staying power. Pack-hunting with long-legged scenthounds, like the Porcelaine, the Ariégeois and the Chien d'Artois, was the main sport of the French nobility in the seventeenth and eighteenth centuries and had reached its zenith prior to the Revolution, careful selective breeding having produced beautifully homogeneous packs with regard to size, conformation, colouring and type of coat. Some were even chosen for strength and harmony of voice! During and after the Revolution, however, many of these packs were unfortunately dispersed and the numbers of hounds decimated, the shorter-legged hounds, such as the various breeds of Bassets, becoming more popular. In England and the United States of America, the Foxhounds, Staghounds and Otterhounds have held sway with riding huntsmen, and the Bassets and Beagles with those who prefer to hunt on foot. In Germany, the Teckel, or Dachshund, has been used in packs, as has even the Sealyham Terrier in Wales, whereas the American Coonhound is, like the Hamiltonstövare, used singly or in couples for the purpose of flushing game. The work of the Bloodhound, the doyen of all scenthounds, is well known to everyone.

There are now about 450 packs of hounds in the United Kingdom whereas in France only a few still exist, among them the well-known Cheverny pack of forty couples of crossed Anglo-French foxhounds, and in Germany there are even fewer. The country which can boast the greatest number of packs is the United States, where it is estimated that together they comprise more than a million dogs, being used for fox-hunting as we know it, as well as trailing and racoon-hunting; in the latter case the hunt takes place at night, the hounds hunting silently through the forest until they scent the quarry, when their baying leads the huntsmen following on foot to the spot where the racoon has been treed. However, the scenthounds generally, with the exception of the Dachshund, Basset, Beagle, Elkhound, Hamiltonstövare and Rhodesian Ridgeback, are less suitable as companions than the sighthounds as their natural instinct to follow a scent overrides everything else, making them sometimes difficult to adapt to the home.

Of the twenty-four dogs in the terrier group, as recognised by the Kennel Club, only one has its origin abroad, namely the Australian Terrier, and even this is descended largely from British breeds. The Romans wrote about the little dogs they found in Britain which pursued fox and badger below ground, and which they named *terrarii* for that reason. The name was abbreviated to *terrars* in Dame Juliana Berners' *Boke* [sic] *of St. Albans*, a list of canines made in the last quarter of the fifteenth century. The first pictorial representation of them is in the Bayeux Tapestry where a couple of little dogs, which could very well be terrier types, can be seen with the hounds in King Harold's hunting party. The modern counterparts of the early terriers are the innumerable hunt terriers which are now bred by the terrier men attached to today's packs, the working terriers which can still face fox, badger, coypu or wild cat without flinching; one need only go to a country sports meeting arranged by hunt supporters in the summer months to see a fine selection of these.

In the sixteenth century, Dr John Caius wrote in his *De Canibus Britannicus* [*Of English Dogges*] of a long-haired, short-legged dog which could only be the forerunner of the present-day Skye Terrier. The Stuart King James VI of Scotland was so enamoured of the little terriers that he sent a few couples of 'earth dogges' from Argyllshire to the King of France at the beginning of the seventeenth century; these must have been early Cairns. The Scottish family of terriers are still the most popular in France, where they are classified in the third group and have their own association, *Le Club des Amateurs de Terriers d'Écosse*. The original terriers from the Western Isles were bred to work the highland cairns and needed long coats for self-protection and long bodies for manoeuvrability; Landseer was the first to feature the Skye Terriers in oil paintings. The Cairn Terrier proper, from the same region of Scotland, being more compact and workmanlike, and having a more manageable coat, has been able to gain and retain a wider popularity. A strain of Cairn-type terrier with light-coloured coats was developed by the Malcolm family of Poltalloch in Argyllshire and evolved as the pure white terrier we know as the West Highland White Terrier, the most eye-catching of the Scottish breeds in our show rings with their coats as white as driven snow. The Scottish Terrier itself differs somewhat in conformation from its three close relatives, the breeder Ian Best of Aberdeen having given it a more powerful muzzle, darker coloration, sturdy conformation and severe character. But the hunting methods of all the terriers of Scotland are the same: to bolt their quarry from the cairns and rocks, or to kill it there if it cannot be dislodged.

The Irish terriers have developed along different lines. With one exception they are long-legged. The short-legged one is the Glen of Imaal. Although one of the oldest terriers of the Emerald Isle, it has only recently been recognised by the English Kennel Club. It was developed in the Glen of Imaal in County Wicklow as a dead game working terrier for hunting fox and badger. It shares the same soft coat texture as the Kerry Blue and the Soft-Coated Wheaten, whereas the red Irish Terrier has a hard coat. All four Irish terriers have been used successfully in otter-hunting. They are all extremely courageous and hard-bitten, the Wheaten being rather less fiery in temperament and more amenable to discipline. They are all certain destroyers of vermin of every kind and the long-legged ones have shown their versatility as gun dogs, herders and guard dogs.

There are only two breeds of terrier which have originated in Wales, namely the Sealyham and the Welsh Terrier. The latter has evolved from the old broken-coated, black-and-tan terrier which has influenced so many breeds. It has been used in the Principality since the eighteenth century with the Ynysfor pack to hunt the strong Welsh hill fox. Although the Welsh huntsmen generally prefer the black-and-tan terriers, the Sealyham is mostly white in colour and short-legged. It was bred in the mid-nineteenth century by Captain John Owen Edwardes, from a variety of broken-coated working terriers, to be dead game to badger, marten and polecat. Sir Jocelyn Lucas even used it in a pack like Beagles after World War 2.

The terriers from the Border, Cheviot and Lake regions have very much in common as to origin and terrain worked. The Border Terrier was developed by the huntsmen of the Border Hunt as a hard game working dog, capable of hunting the grey hill fox on the rocky slopes of the Cheviots. It had to have the stamina to run for miles with the hounds and the courage to bolt its quarry when cornered. Its medium-length legs enable it to do this and to go to ground when necessary. Among its ancestors are the Dandie Dinmont, Bedlington and Lakeland, all noted for their toughness and great spirit. The Dandie Dinmonts were the favourites of the Romany wanderers of those parts, who used them against fox, badger and wild cat, and the Bedlingtons from the same origins were taken up by the miners of Northumbria and used primarily for rabbiting and ratting. The Lakeland Terrier was evolved by Cumberland and Westmorland huntsmen from local black-and-tan Patterdale working terriers, with an admixture of Bedlington/Dandie/Welsh and Fox Terrier blood, and worked in the same way as the Border.

The English terriers as such form the biggest sub-group. The Airedale from the Yorkshire area around Bingley and Otley is the most imposing of all terriers. An intrepid hunter of otter and badger in the vales of York, it has proved its worth as a superb guard and patrol dog. At the other extreme, we have the diminutive Norfolk and Norwich Terriers, small in size but great in heart, one-time favourites of Cambridge University students. The Fox Terriers, both Smooth- and Wire-Coated, are of course the classic English terriers of fox-hunting in the show rings, their more workaday cousins, the Jack Russells, not yet being admitted to such august places except at specially-organised hunt events. The Manchester Terrier is the ratting dog *par excellence* and as a rabbiter it has few equals; as a show dog it appeals to the purists who seek perfection in both conformation and coloration. We come finally to the Bull Terriers (White, Coloured, Miniature and Stafford), all evolved from the bull-and-terrier types of the early nineteenth century. Bred originally for bull-baiting and later for the dog-fighting pits, they have been refined over the years into show dogs of distinction; the Staffies having topped the terrier entries more than once at Crufts.

The Australian Terrier is the odd man out as far as the Kennel Club grouping is concerned. A true terrier of smallest stature, it is rightly classified in this group as it makes an excellent killer of small vermin and a fine sharp-eared watch dog for the home, greatly appreciated 'down under' and deservedly growing in popularity in this country.

Hounds

Afghan Hound

When prepared for the show ring, where it is extremely popular today, the Afghan Hound is at the peak of its glamour; no wonder it has repeatedly been used as an exotic photographic model in the company of the most beautiful mannequins of top couturiers such as Dior, Balmain and Schiaparelli. One of the oldest of the sighthounds, it is said to date back thousands of years B.C. and, indeed, dogs of similar appearance do appear in cave paintings of the period.

Ch Montravia Kaskarak Hitari, by Ch Sacheverell Zukwala, ex Nosilla I'm a Smartee, br Mrs L. Race, pr Mrs P. Gibbs

It is a dignified and majestic dog of proud, arrogant bearing and seems to personify the beauty of speed; when in repose, its steady, far-seeing, detached gaze is pervaded by the mystery of the East. Along with the Saluki of Persia and the Sloughi of North Africa, it is the only dog allowed to sleep in the tents of the nomadic tribes who wander across the arid regions of Persia, Syria and Afghanistan. It is allotted one of their valuable carpets for a bed and it has been reported that, when a bitch is unable to feed her offspring, it is not uncommon for a tribeswoman feeding her own child to share her milk with the puppies!

The Afghan Hound has a longer, warmer coat than its cousins further South, a necessary protection against the freezing cold of the plains, hills and passes of its native country. It has been used down the ages for hunting gazelle, antelope and wolf; mounted tribesmen would release a falcon which had been trained to dive onto the head of the quarry, when the hounds would give chase and finally catch hold of the exhausted beast until the huntsmen arrived to dispatch it. It has also been used as a herder and guard dog for the itinerant flocks of sheep and goats.

Specimens of the breed were brought to Europe and the United States of America early in this century; a breed club was formed in England in 1926 and standards were drawn up by the English and American Kennel Clubs at the same time, only to be revised in 1948. It was not until after World War 2 that it became established on the Continent. As one of the family, it shows great faithfulness and affection towards the other members, but it is aloof towards strangers and requires firm handling when in the formative stages. It is well behaved in the house, but must have a vigorous daily workout off the lead to keep it in top condition, as well as regular brushing to preserve the beauty of its coat. In the ring, its magnificent coat, together with its smooth, springy gait and aristocratic mien, distinguish it as a dog of the highest style.

The head has a long skull of moderate width and a prominent occiput. It is crowned with a topknot. The foreface is long, the stop only slight and the jaws powerful with a level mouth. The eyes are preferably dark but can be golden; nearly triangular, they have an oriental slant upwards from the inner corner. The nose is usually black but can be liver in light-coloured dogs. The ears are set low and well back, being carried close to the head. They are covered with long silky hair. The neck is long and strong, carrying the head proudly.

Forequarters have long sloping shoulders, well set back and well muscled. Forelegs are straight with good bone. They are in line with the shoulders, the elbows being held in. The back is well muscled, level and of moderate length, falling slightly to the stern. The shortish loin is straight and broad. Hip bones are rather prominent and set wide apart. The chest is deep and the ribs fairly well sprung. Hindquarters are powerful with well-bent and well-turned stifles. The distance between hip and hock is comparatively much longer than between hock and foot. Removal of dewclaws is discretionary.

The feet are covered with long thick hair. Forefeet are strong and large with arched toes. Pasterns are long and springy, especially in front.

Hindfeet are long but not so broad as the forefeet. The tail is of moderate length, set on low and with a ring at the end. It is lightly feathered and raised in action.

The eye-catching coat is long and of fine texture on ribs, fore- and hindquarters, and flanks. The hair of mature dogs is long on the head from the forehead backwards with a silky topknot, but short on the foreface and short and close from the shoulders backwards along the saddle. Ears and legs are well covered, but pasterns can be bare. All colours are acceptable.

For the first time ever an Afghan was supreme champion at Crufts in 1983; he was the brindle dog, Ch. Montravia Kaskarak Hitari, owned by Mrs Pauline Gibbs. The popularity of the Afghan as both pet and show dog is illustrated by the fact that this breed again topped the breed entries for 1983. Indeed 2 days after the Crufts win, another Afghan, Ch. Kabiks the Challenger, took supreme honours at the top Westminster Show, New York, for his owners Chris and Marguerite Terrell. This winning streak in 1983 was continued in Australia at the Sydney Royal Show, won by Ch. Calahorra Boccacio for owners J. Blunden and S. and W. Slatyer.

Height: dogs 27 – 29 in (69 – 74 cm); bitches 24 – 26 in (61 – 66 cm).
Weight: relative to height.

Basenji

Unusual in several respects, the Basenji is best known as the barkless dog; instead of barking it emits a kind of plaintive chuckling noise. It does, however, growl and whine like other dogs. As a pack-hunter, it has been trained to work silently for centuries and some blame this for its inability to give voice. Another unusual feature is its way of washing, in cat fashion, by licking its paws; it is in fact a member of the Spitz group, some of which tend also to wash in this way, and it is fastidiously clean.

It is one of the most ancient of breeds, going back to prehistoric times, originating, it is thought, among the Ituri pygmies in the forests of the Sudan. The Egyptian Pharaohs adopted the little hunting dog for themselves and indeed prized it to such an extent that we find it represented in carvings on the friezes of tombs of the fourth dynasty. It is usually depicted lying near the couch of its master. Archaeologists call it the dog of Cheops, after the Pharaoh of that dynasty who built the great pyramid.

All traces of the Basenji were lost after that age until the early 1870s, when the breed was rediscovered by white explorers in the forest lands between the Congo and the Sudan, where the natives were found to be using it again as a pack-hunting dog. A bell would be fastened to its collar for location purposes when working and its job was to drive game into a wide net. It was also used as a guard.

Its name means 'bush dog'. It is believed to belong to a breed that has naturally evolved from the jackal; there are similar dogs to be found in Africa but only the Basenji is barkless, proving its pure breeding, since puppies from Basenji crosses do bark. In 1895, a couple of Basenjis were imported to England, but it was not until 1937 that one appeared at Crufts under the name African Bush Dog or Congo Terrier. Early imports had been decimated by distemper but the breed began to become established just before World War 2, new stock having been imported from the Sudan. A standard was drawn up in South Africa in 1939 and revised by the Basenji Club of Great Britain in 1942. Since the war, it has not looked back and is now a firm favourite with showgoers and those who appreciate a dog which is different. It is an excellent house dog and loves plenty of exercise; having an affinity with horses, it will accompany a rider for miles.

Another unusual feature is that the bitch comes into season once a year only, often in late autumn or early winter. The Basenji is a good family dog, very gentle with children and devoid of odour. It can also be very droll at times, somewhat mischievous and cold towards strangers, and with a cat-like independence, yet it is very affectionate and faithful to its own family. Although it is still used for hunting in Africa, it is more a show dog and

Ch Neyeliz Castanea, by Fula Kweku of the Congo, ex Ch Neyeliz Anabela Charlotte, brs Mr & Mrs S. Smith, pr Mr K. J. Richardson

companion in Europe. Another peculiarity is its dislike of water, either as rain or even to drink. Its wrinkled brow seems to go very well with the curiosity it displays in everything going on around it.

The head has a flat skull of moderate width, which tapers towards the nose, and a slight stop. The distance from the top of the head to the stop is a little more than from the stop to the tip of the nose. Wrinkles appear on the forehead when the ears are pricked; the wrinkles are more noticeable in puppies. The nose is preferably black. The eyes are almond-shaped, inscrutable and set obliquely. The ears are pointed, erect, of fine texture and set well forward. The mouth is strong with scissor bite, the upper incisors slightly overlapping and touching the lower. The neck is strong, of good length, and well crested; it is set into well-laid-back shoulders giving the head a proud carriage.

Forequarters are muscular with slender shoulder blades, close at the withers, and elbows firmly tucked in against the brisket and in line with the ribs. The forelegs are straight and finely boned, with flexible pasterns. The back is short and level and the ribs well sprung, deep and oval. The loin is short-coupled and the deep brisket turns up into a definite waist. Hindquarters are strong and muscular, with hocks well let down, long second thighs and moderately bent stifles.

Feet are small, narrow and compact with deep pads and well-arched toes. The tail is set high with the curve of the buttock extending beyond its root; it curls tightly over the spine and lies closely to the thigh with a single or double curl. The coat is short, sleek, very fine, close and silky. The colour is bright red, jet black or black-and-tan, all having white feet, chest and tail tip. Optional are white legs, white blaze and white collar.

Height: dogs 16–18 in (41–46 cm); bitches 15–17 in (38–43 cm).
Weight: dogs 24 lb (11 kg); bitches 21 lb (9.5 kg).

Basset Hound

Like the Bloodhound, which it very closely resembles as far as the head is concerned, the Basset Hound has its origins in France in the early fifteenth century. The French historian, de Fouilloux, in his hunting book, *La Vénerie*, written in the latter half of the sixteenth century, tells of a low Basset-type dog, with crooked forelegs, popular at that time in the province of Artois; this is the dog which came to be known later as the Basset Artésien Normand. Prior to the Revolution of 1789, the aristocrats, who always rode to the hunt, had preferred long-legged hounds, but many kennels were dispersed during the Revolution and, in subsequent years, the low-to-ground

Ch Lodway Lancer of Islwyn, by Ch Langpool Carries Lad of Islwyn, ex Ch Mayflower of Langpool, br Miss P. Flynn, prs Mr & Mrs J. W. R. Roberts

dogs, which could be followed on foot by huntsmen with guns, gradually took the place of long-legged hounds, although many of the latter still remain, such as the fine pack at the Château de Cheverny in the Loire Valley. Breeding programmes, which favoured the short-legged dogs as being slower and more suitable for hunting smaller animals than deer, resulted in several varieties, including the rough-haired Basset Fauve de Bretagne and Basset Griffon Vendéen, and the smooth-haired Basset Bleu de Gascogne and Basset Artésien Normand, the latter being carefully bred and developed by the Comte le Coulteux de Canteleu, who did so much for the Bloodhound. It is the Artésien variety that contributed most to the Basset Hound as we know it today. It was first presented in 1863 in Paris, at the first dog show held in that city. A few years later, Lord Galway acquired a few couples for his breeding kennels and some of these he passed on to Lord Onslow, but it was Sir John Everett Millais who did most for the breed in Britain; his imported stud dog Model was not only the first Basset shown here at Wolverhampton in 1873, but also the cornerstone of his most successful breeding programme. Model was the outstanding dog of his time, and was used by Sir John, first by crossing with the Beagle and the Artésien and later the Bloodhound, to produce a fine strain of hounds; the outcross with the Bloodhound had to be achieved by artificial insemination due to natural physical problems, Sir John being a pioneer in this field.

After the Basset Hound was recognised by the Kennel Club in 1880 and a breed club was formed in 1884, its popularity grew rapidly in the hunting field, as well as in the show ring. The first pack to be formed was the Heseltines' Walhampton in 1891, followed by others as the value of the slow hound became better appreciated. The two World Wars had serious effects on breeding but the Basset flag was kept flying, after the first, by Mrs Elms' Reynalton Kennel and after the second by Miss Keevil's Grims Kennel. The Basset Hound Club was revived in 1954 after a lapse of 30 years or so. The breed has not looked back since and today it is considered one of the most fascinating of show dogs.

Although very slow and deliberate, the Basset Hound is an effective scenthound and, having once found the scent of a hare, rarely loses it; as with the Bloodhound, the trail does not necessarily have to be recent, such is its keenness of nose. However, although it is not often hunted these days, and only the lighter-weight dogs are suitable for this purpose, it has made a great impression in the show rings of the world where the heavyweights have had notable successes. Its wonderful temperament is one of the principal reasons for its success. Despite its great size, it makes a good family companion, but does require plenty of room in the house, its long, always-wagging tail being rather prone to knocking things off coffee tables. Its mournful expression, however, seems to solicit our sympathy and one is compelled to forgive its failings and rather queer appearance, even when it runs away when called and returns all in its own good time when it has come to the end of some fascinating trail. These characteristics are nowhere more vividly portrayed than in the *Daily Mail* comic strip-cartoon *Fred Basset*, by Alex Graham, and advertisements for 'Hush Puppy' shoes have made its appearance familiar to all.

In the show ring, its action is considered an important point; a smooth free action is required with forelegs reaching well forward and hindlegs showing powerful thrust. It must move true both front and rear. Hocks and stifles must not be stiff in movement and toes must not be dragged.

The head is domed with a prominent occiput. It is fairly wide at the brow, with a moderate stop and a tapering slightly to the muzzle, the foreface being generally lean but not snipy. The line from the tip of the nose to the stop is almost parallel with that from the stop to the occiput and not much longer. The skin of the head is loose and wrinkles when drawn forward or when the head is lowered. The upper flews overlap the lower. The nose is usually large and black but can be brown or liver in light-coloured hounds. The eyes are brown or shading to hazel in light-coloured dogs, with the haw showing a little. The ears (leathers) are set fairly low, never above the eyeline; they are very long, reaching to the end of the muzzle, narrow and curling inwards, and their texture is supple, fine and velvety. The mouth is very strong with scissor bite, but pincer bite is not a fault. The neck is muscular and fairly long with good dewlap.

18

Forequarters have well-laid-back shoulder-blades and short, powerful forelegs with great bone. The elbows fit easily against the side and the knees are slightly crooked inwards but without touching each other. Knuckling over is a bad fault. The skin between knee and foot may be wrinkled. The breast bone protrudes slightly, but the chest is not narrow or unduly deep. The ribs are well rounded and sprung.

The back is rather broad and level and not too long and the withers and quarters are at the same height. The loins may arch slightly. Hindquarters are very muscular and well rounded when viewed from behind. The stifles are well bent and the hocks low to ground, bending under the body and pointing forward.

Feet are massive, well knuckled up and padded. Forefeet may point ahead or turn slightly out, but in either case the dog must stand perfectly true, leaving the imprint of a large hound. The tail is well set on, long, strong at the base and tapering, with a moderate amount of coarse hair underneath. In movement, the stern curves gently in sabre fashion over the back, carried well up, but not curling or gay.

The coat is smooth, short and close, but not fine; the outline is clean and free from feathering. The colour is usually tricolour — black, white and tan — or lemon and white; any other hound colour is acceptable.

Height: 13–15 in (33–38 cm). The American standard stipulates a height not exceeding 14 in (35-36 cm).
Weight: relative to height.

Beagle

Although references to small hounds, similar to Beagles and used for hunting the hare on foot, are to be found in ancient writings, it is not until much later that we find them called by name. In the privy accounts of Henry VIII, there is a mention of a payment to Robert Shere, 'Keper of the Begles', for their care and food. James I's pet name for his Queen was 'little Beagle', and, in the mid-seventeenth century, Sir Arthur Bryant describes, in his *Life of Charles II*, how much the monarch enjoyed hunting hare on Newmarket Heath accompanied by his pack of Beagles. At about the same time Pope wrote:

'To plain with well-bred Beagles we repair,
And trace the mazes of the circling hare'.

In the eighteenth century, William III is reported to have enjoyed Beagle-hunting and George IV is known also to have kept a pack. Beagles of a type closely resembling those we see today are depicted in a coloured plate in Sydenham Edwards' *Cynographia Britannica* published in 1800, and by

Ch & Am Ch Graadtre's Hot Pursuit of Rossut, by Am Ch Starbucks Hang 'Em High, ex Am Ch Plain and Fancy's Delilah, brs Mr & Mrs Hammes, pr Miss P. A. Sutton

artists such as Stubbs, Herring and the Barrauds. It is not surprising that, with such royal favour shown to the breed, the aristocracy and sportsmen in general followed suit and beagling became one of their favourite pastimes. The sport was quickly taken up abroad, on the Continent and in North America. Although used mostly to hunt hare, Beagles have been used against jackal in Africa and wild boar and small deer in Ceylon; the Scandinavians have also used them for deer-hunting and Americans and Canadians have even used them as gun dogs.

A variety known as the Pocket Beagle, measuring under 10 in (25.4 cm) at the withers and obtained by selective breeding-down from small examples, became popular for rabbit-hunting in the sixteenth century. Elizabeth I is said to have been very keen on it and to have had a few couples carried around with her in a large pannier on a mule's back in case she fancied a bit of sport on her journeys! This small variety went out of fashion in the seventeenth century but was revived in the eighteenth century, only to decline again towards the end of the nineteenth century as the larger variety was more able to stand up to a day's hard work over rough terrain.

Beagling is a popular sport today, appealing as it does to a wider circle than fox-hunting, if only because it is not necessary to ride. After the usual cup

20

outside the pub or farmhouse where the meet is held, the hounds move off, fanning out ahead of the Master and whippers-in in their smart green livery, followed by the field, all of them on foot, eyes peeled for the first sight of a brown hare. When a scent is picked up, the already-feathering tails are joined by loud baying and the chase is on, with hounds in full cry to the sound of the horn.

The Beagle Club was formed in 1890 and a breed standard drawn up, specifying a smallish tough hound, able to hunt the hare in a workmanlike manner. The standard has changed little over the years, the principal variable being the height and this depended, as far as packs were concerned, on the terrain to be worked. The club staged its first show in 1896, and later shows were held annually, but the show Beagle did not really take off until 1931 when twenty-seven dogs were registered at the Kennel Club and Challenge Certificates were on offer at four shows. Although World War 2 caused some packs to be disbanded or reduced in numbers, the Beagle picked up again afterwards and, in the 1950s, the number of championship shows increased. Ch. Barvae Statute was the first Beagle to go Best in Show at an all-breed championship show and his daughter, Ch. Derawuda Vixen, was best bitch at Crufts in 1959; by this time, the well-known Rozavel Kennel, belonging to Mrs Thelma Gray of Welsh Corgi fame, was well established and producing superb show stock.

Today the Beagle is one of the smartest of its group. It is described as a merry, sturdy, compact hound, giving an impression of quality. The head is fairly long, powerful in the male but finer in the female, and free from frown or wrinkle. The skull is slightly domed and moderately wide. The distance between the occiput and the well-defined stop is about the same as that between the stop and the tip of the black, broad nose. Light-coloured hounds can have a lighter-pigmented nose. Eyes are dark or hazel and fairly large, set well apart. Ears are long, round-tipped and set on low, hanging gracefully. They are of fine texture and reach the nose when pulled forward. Teeth are strong with scissor bite, upper incisors just overlapping and touching the lower. The neck is long enough to allow the dog to scent easily and slightly arched with a little dewlap.

Forequarters have sloping shoulders and straight, well-boned forelegs, set well under. Pasterns are short and elbows held firmly against the sides. The height to elbow is half that to withers. The chest is well let down and body topline is level. Ribs are well sprung, extending well back; they are short between the couplings. The loins are powerful and supple. Hindquarters have muscular thighs and well-bent stifles. Hocks are firm, well let down and parallel.

The feet are tight and firm, well knuckled up with strong pads. The tail is thick at the root, sturdy and of moderate length, set on high and carried gaily but not over the back. It is well covered with hair, especially underneath, and white-tipped. The coat is short, dense and weatherproof and of any hound colour except liver. When the dog is on the move, the back is level and without roll and the stride is straight, free and long-reaching with driving hindlegs.

Height: dogs 15–16 in (38–40 cm); bitches 13–15 in (33–38 cm). In the USA two heights are specified: (1) Not exceeding 13 in (33 cm); (2) Over 13 in but not exceeding 15 in (over 33 but not exceeding 38 cm).
Weight: relative to height.

Bloodhound

Known as the Bloodhound in the English-speaking world and as the Saint-Hubert in Belgium, France and Switzerland, this fine breed of scenthounds (*Canis sagaces*) is thought to have descended from the running dogs of ancient Gaul, which were used to hunt wild ox and boar and were mentioned by Greek and Roman writers of the second century; the statue of Diana in the Louvre Museum represents the Goddess of the Hunt with four of these hounds at her feet. In mediaeval times, it shared popularity with greyhound types and mastiffs and we see it depicted in pictures of that era. The Bishop of Liège in Belgium, who died in A.D.727, was a great huntsman and had brought his pack of hounds with him from Aquitaine in France, where he was born. When he was canonized as Saint-Hubert, he became the patron saint of the hunter. After his death, the pack was transferred to the Abbey of Andin in the Ardennes, where the saint's relics are deposited and from where the monks used to send three couples yearly to the French Court. The monks jealously kept on the breed in honourable memory of the saint who had hunted with Saint-Eustache. However, Charles IX found them too slow-moving for the chase and replaced them in 1570 by faster white dogs, keeping the Saint-Hubert hounds for tracking purposes only.

The hound was brought to England by William the Conqueror in 1066, where it was renamed the Bloodhound because of its great skill in tracking a wounded animal by following a trail left by its drops of blood. This skill was utilised later by police in the West for tracking missing persons and criminals and in the Southern States of America for apprehending escaping slaves; its part in these activities has been much distorted in literature as it would rarely harm anyone it caught; more often than not it would show him great affection with a vigorous licking from its huge tongue! Walt Disney portrays the funny side of the Bloodhound in his lovable character Pluto. As a police tracker, the Bloodhound has now been replaced by the German Shepherd.

Ch Herdus Buttercup, by Ch Brightons Questor, ex Ch Brightons Ladybird, brs/prs Mr & Mrs R. A. Hutchinson

Napoleon III had a dozen couples in his pack kennelled at Meudon, and one of the last packs in France was owned by Comte le Coulteux de Canteleu, but the Bloodhound's prowess as a hunter is neglected today. It has been especially influential as a progenitor of many fine breeds, such as the Otterhound, the Bruno du Jura and the American Black-and-Tan Coonhound featured so dramatically in the chase of a Siberian snow tiger in the film *When the North Wind Blows*, and also of low-to-ground dogs, to a greater or lesser extent, like the Basset Artésien Normand, the Basset Hound, the Dachsbracke and hence, eventually, the Dachshund.

Its temperament is one of the friendliest of all scenthounds, towards both people and canines; it is attached to its owner and loves children, but needs plenty of room and good exercise to be happy. Although not a guard dog, its loud bark acts as a deterrent. It possesses, to the highest degree, all the

23

attributes of the dog that hunts by scent. Its expression is noble and dignified, characterised by solemnity, wisdom and power, whilst being at the same time of a somewhat reserved and sensitive nature. It is a massive dog of slow but imposing carriage; it is also slow to anger but should not be provoked.

The head is characteristic of the breed. It is narrow in proportion to length and long in proportion to the body, tapering only slightly from the temples to the muzzle. In profile, the upper outline of the skull is nearly in the same plane as that of the foreface. The stop is midway between the tip of the nose and the occiput. The overall length of the head from nose tip to occiput is not less than 12 in (30 cm) in dogs and 11 in (28 cm) in bitches. The skull is long and narrow with prominent occiput. The foreface is long, deep, of even width and with a square outline in profile. The head is covered with a thin loose skin, which falls in loose pendulous ridges and folds over the forehead and cheeks when the head is carried low. The nostrils are large and wide. In front, the lips fall squarely, making a right angle with the upper line of the foreface, whilst behind they form deep hanging flews and continue into the sagging folds of loose skin on the neck to form a very pronounced dewlap. The eyes are deep set and sunk into the orbits, the lids being of lozenge shape, the lower lids dragged down by the heavy flews and showing a dark red mucous membrane (the haw). In colour, they match the overall colour of the dog, varying from deep hazel to yellow; hazel is preferred but seldom seen in liver-and-tan or red-and-tan hounds. The ears are thin and soft to touch, very long, set on low and falling in graceful folds, the lower parts arching inwards and backwards. The bite is scissor, the upper incisors overlapping the lower. The nose is black and the neck is long.

Forequarters have muscular shoulders which slope well back. Forelegs are straight, large and round in bone, with elbows squarely set and strong pasterns. The ribs are well sprung and the chest well let down, forming a deep keel. The back and loins are strong, the latter deep and slightly arched. Hindquarters have very muscular thighs and second thighs and the hocks are well bent, let down and squarely cut.

The feet are round, strong and well knuckled up. The tail is long and thick and carried like a scimitar, but not curled over the back or in corkscrew fashion. It is set on high with a fair amount of hair underneath which gets shorter towards the end. The coat is short and fairly hard on the body but soft and silky on ears and skull. The colours are black-and-tan (preferably), liver-and-tan, red-and-tan or self-coloured red. The darker colours are sometimes interspersed with lighter or badger-coloured hair, or flecked with white. Touches of white are allowed on chest, feet and end of tail.

Height: dogs 25–27 in (63–69 cm); bitches 23–25 in (58–63 cm).
Weight: dogs up to 110 lb (50 kg); bitches up to 100 lb (45 kg).

Borzoi

A hound from the steppes of Russia, the Borzoi or Rouskaïa Psowaya Barsaya as it is known in its native land, the ancient wolfhound of the Tsars, is now what many believe to be the most beautiful of all show dogs. It has its roots in the original Russian sighthounds and the Caucasian running dogs which accompanied migrating tribes, and it is on record that long-haired dogs of similar appearance existed in Russia in the eleventh century. When Henri I of France married Anne, daughter of Yaroslav the Wise, she brought with her three Borzois, the first to come to Western Europe. The original types had been so improved by selective breeding by the Tartars and later by the aristocracy of the Imperial Russian Court, where hundreds of couples were kept, that dogs described in documents of the time are clearly recognisable as Borzois. In 1519, King Christian of Denmark gave a couple to Francis I and, in a book of hours, Vassili Ivanovitch, father of Ivan the Terrible and Grand Duke of Moscow, is depicted on a pilgrimage with three of these dogs at his side.

Ch Stonebar Reflection of Ryazan, by Ch Stonebar Nikolenka, ex Francehill Full Hand, br Mrs G. Ross, pr Miss J. Clarke

In the seventeenth and eighteenth centuries, wolf-hunting and hare-coursing were favourite pastimes of the nobility and stud books were opened in order to arrive at a definitive type, as two varieties had evolved, a shorter-haired one in Central and Southern Russia (the Tchistopsovaya) and a longer-haired, fuller-coated one in the North (the Goustopsovaya); these had their subdivisions making seven types in all. When Alexander II freed the serfs in 1861, interest in the chase waned progressively and many estates were split up with consequent dispersal of packs of hounds. But, in 1873, a Borzoi Hunt Club was formed with the object of preserving the breed and its purpose in hunting wolf, fox and hare, and the first show took place in the same year. A standard was drawn up and selective breeding intensified, merging the different types and distilling them into one magnificent refined animal such as we have today, with the strain of the Grand Duke Nicolai Nicolayevitch exerting great influence. By the end of the nineteenth century, it was beginning to be seen at European shows, where it attracted great attention. When the Tsar gave Queen Alexandra a few couples, the seal was put on its passport to success throughout the world. To see it moving gracefully and majestically round the ring, resplendent in its coat of silk and gold, supremely elegant, is a memorable experience.

It is endowed with keen sight, exceptional intelligence and a good, although reserved, temperament. It makes an excellent guard dog; indeed it unexpectedly took first prize in the world competition for defence at Houston, Texas, in 1974. It is perhaps for this innate ability and still latent instincts of the wolfhound that it needs to be supervised when at play with young children. It needs a good workout off the lead every day and a large enclosed garden where it can be at liberty if it is to reach fulfilment and true potential. It is a dog of outstanding courage, muscular power and great speed over short distances.

Its head is long, lean and well filled in below the eyes. The inner corner of the eye is equidistant to the occiput and the tip of the nose. The skull is narrow and slightly domed, with imperceptible stop, inclining to a Roman nose. The head is so fine that the direction of the bones and principal veins can be seen. The jaws are long, deep and powerful with scissor bite. The nose is large, black and rounded. The skull tapers gradually to the nose. The eyes are dark and keen, almond-shaped, set obliquely and placed well back but not too far apart. The eye rims are dark. The ears are small, fine and mobile, and moderately separated. The neck is slightly arched and fairly long, well set on and flat at the sides.

Forequarters have clean shoulders sloping well back, fine at the withers. Forelegs are lean and straight; when seen frontally they are narrow and, in profile, they are wide at the shoulder, narrowing to the foot. Elbows turn neither in nor out and pasterns are strong and flexible. The chest is narrow with great depth of brisket. Ribs are well sprung, neither flat-sided nor barrel-shaped, and very deep, providing plenty of room for heart and lungs. The back rises in an arch from near the shoulder to a well-balanced fall-away. The muscles are well distributed and developed. Hindquarters have broad, powerful loins with good muscularity. Quarters are wider than shoulders, giving a stable stance. The thighs are long and well developed with good second thighs. Hindlegs are long and muscular, with well-bent stifles and well-let-down broad hocks.

The forefeet are rather long with toes close together, well arched and pointing forward. Hindfeet are hare-like, longer and less arched. The tail is long, rather low set and carried low; in action it does not rise above the level of the back, and from hock level it may be sickle-shaped but not ringed.

The coat is long and silky, or flat, wavy or curly. It is short and smooth on the head, ears and front legs, with a profuse and rather curly frill on the neck. Forelegs and chest are well feathered, as are the hindquarters and tail. The colours are white, all the golden colours, gold shaded with silver or with dark points, sable, grey, brindle, red, black. In dark-coloured dogs, a black mask is usual. All the colours can be self or over a white ground. In self colours, the shade is darkest on the back and gets lighter towards the extremities and the back of the legs. The Tsars are said to have preferred the light colours. In movement, it takes great supple strides. In the chase, it proceeds at a steady trot until the flushing of the game, then it breaks into a fast gallop as it leaps forward in pursuit.

Height: dogs not less than 29 in (74 cm); bitches not less than 27 in (68 cm).
Weight: relative to height.

Dachshunds

The Dachshund was bred specifically to hunt badger and fox in the forests of Germany, where it is known as the Teckel. There are three varieties, Smooth-Haired, Long-Haired and Wire-Haired, and two sizes, Standard and Miniature. On the Continent, a smaller third size is recognised, the Kaninchen-teckel (maximum weight 3.5 kg [7.7 lb]; 30 cm [11.8 in] girth measurement), used for rabbit-catching. The Dachs is said to date back to the Bavarian Bibarhund of the seventh century, but the name Teckel, or Dachshund, was not known until centuries later. Outcrossing clearly took place and the French Braque, the Austrian Dachsbracke, and the German Pinscher were all used at one time or another to produce what we know today as the Dachshund.

In 1845, Prince Albert acquired a few couples from Prince Edward of Saxe-Weimar and brought them to Windsor, where he used them to flush

(Miniature Smooth-Haired) Ch Pipersvale Pina-Colada, by Ch Monksmile Dan-De-Lion, ex Pipersvale Beaujolais, br/pr Mrs B. Munt

(Standard Long-Haired) Ch Loggeta Flower Power, by Africandawns Beau Louis, ex Ch Africandawns Boobs of Loggeta, brs/prs Mr & Mrs Cross

pheasants in Windsor Forest. Queen Victoria was soon captivated by the strange little dogs and set up a breeding kennel for them. Prince Edward, later Edward VII, also took a great interest in them and won first prize with a black-and-tan at the Crystal Palace Show in 1875. The Queen received the second prize! The breed was now becoming popular and a breed club was formed in England in 1881 with the aim of improving type; in Germany a stud book was opened in 1890 and the standard drawn up.

The long-haired Dachs did not arrive until halfway through the nineteenth century. It was the result of careful crossing of the Smooth-Haired variety with the German Spaniel and the Stöberhund at the kennels of the Bavarian

(Miniature Wire-Haired) Ch Drakesleat Rags t' Riches, by Drakesleat Range Rover, ex Ch Drakesleat Casey's Court, br Mrs Z. Andrews, prs Mrs Z. Andrews & Mr J. Horswell

Court, a happy combination producing the beautiful animal of today. It was not imported here until 1920, when five were registered, but it had not been an easy time for the breed in general during World War 1, when things German and their national dog were an anathema to many people and stocks became depleted, a reaction which occurred also in World War 2.

The Wire-Haired variety was the last of the three to evolve. It resulted from a cross of the Smooth-Haired Dachshund with the small Wire-Haired Schnauzer, the Czesky terrier and the Dandie Dinmont, in order to give it a tougher coat more suitable for hunting in rough terrain. It did not take on in England until the first quarter of this century; in 1927, the Wire-Haired Dachshund Club was formed and, at the 1928 Crufts show, Lady Berwick went Best of Breed with her Wire-Haired dog. Much excellent stock had been introduced in all three varieties and sound foundations laid for the breed.

One of the most popular of hound breeds, the Dachshund is an intelligent and obedient little dog and very adaptable; it is as much at home in a city flat as in a country house and its loud deep bark, not unlike that of the Dandie Dinmont, makes it an ideal watch dog. It has proved itself immensely valuable to the sportsman, especially abroad, against badger, fox, otter, and rabbit, its short legs allowing it to go to ground with ease like a terrier, whilst for tracking and field work its keen nose is one of the best.

In literature, it appears in Dr Axel Münthe's *Story of San Michele*; when the doctor was looking upon the Neckar Valley from the terrace of the old ruined castle of Heidelberg, a Dachshund puppy rushed up to him.

'His cunning eyes had discovered my secret at the first glance. My secret was that I had always been longing to possess just such a little Waldmann. . . . Hard up though I was I bought Waldmann at once for fifty marks and we returned in triumph to the hôtel, Waldmann trotting close to my heels without a leash, quite certain that his master was I and nobody else.'

In the art form of the strip-cartoon, everyone will recall the adventures of heroine Jane and her smooth Dachshund called Fritz in the *Daily Mirror*.

The three varieties are identical in conformation and colour, the variations being in coat and size, but if one looks for differences in character, the Smooth can be said to be the liveliest and especially intelligent, the Long-Haired the most elegant, calm and engaging, and the Wire-Haired the toughest and most workmanlike — differences due to the characteristics of the outcrosses used. The general appearance is that of a long but compact, short-legged dog, strong and well muscled, with good carriage.

The head is long and conical seen from above and sharp and finely modelled in profile, tapering to the tip of the nose. The skull is of moderate width, slightly arched in profile, with a moderate stop and sloping to a slightly arched muzzle. The foreface is long and narrow and the jaw strong, opening wide. The lips are tightly stretched, the upper lip neatly covering the lower jaw. The eyes are oval, of medium size and set obliquely. They are dark in colour, except in the case of chocolates when they may be lighter; in dapples, one or both may be wall eyes. The ears are broad, rounded and of moderate length. They are very mobile, set high and relatively well back, lying close to the cheek. When pulled forward, they reach to halfway between the eyes and the tip of nose. The teeth are strong and the bite scissor, the upper incisors fitting closely over the lower. The neck is fairly long and muscular without dewlap, slightly arched in the nape and running gracefully into the shoulders; it carries the head erect in a bold manner.

Forequarters are muscular with deep oval chest and prominent breast bone, long broad shoulders set firmly and obliquely on a well-developed rib cage. The upper arm is equal in length and at right angles to the shoulder blade. The elbows lie close to the ribs and move freely up to the shoulder blades. The forearm is comparatively short, inclined slightly inwards forming the crook, and when seen in profile is fairly straight; it must not bend forward or knuckle over. The forelegs should cover the lowest point of the breastline when looked at from the side; they are very short and well boned. The back is generally level, the topline only slightly depressed over the shoulders and slightly arched over the short loin, and parallel to the ground. The belly is moderately tucked up. Hindquarters have a round rump, with pelvic bone not too short and set obliquely, and a strong thigh bone jointed at right angles to the pelvis. The lower thigh is short, set at right angles to the upper thigh, and well muscled. The hocks are set wide apart, well developed, and the legs straight and parallel viewed from behind.

The forefeet are full, broad and straight or turned slightly outwards. Hindfeet are smaller and narrower and, in the Wire-Haired, are placed straight. The toes are compact and arched with strong nails and firm pads. The tail is set on fairly high, strong, tapering, not too long, too curved or carried too high. The colours are black-and-tan, dark brown with lighter shadings, dark red, light red, dappled, tiger-marked, brindle or chocolate. A white spot on the chest is admissible. Dapple dogs should be evenly dappled. Nose and nails should be black, but in chocolates and dapples the nose may be brown or flesh coloured.

The coat of the Smooth-Haired Dachs is short, dense, smooth and strong. The hair under the tail is coarse. The skin is loose and supple, fitting closely without much wrinkle. The coat of the Long-Haired variety is soft and straight or slightly waved and glossy. It is longer under the neck, under the body and particularly on the ears and behind the legs, where it develops into feathering. It reaches its greatest length on the tail, where it forms a flag. The feathering extends to the outside of the ears. It is an elegant coat resembling that of the Irish Setter. The coat of the Wire-Haired, except on the jaw, eyebrows and ears, is completely even, short and harsh, with a softer undercoat. The chin is bearded, the eyebrows bushy and the ears smooth.

The three Miniature Dachshunds are similar in conformation to the Standard varieties in all respects except size. Any appearance of toyishness is to be avoided. Other points being equal, the smaller the better, but type and soundness take precedence over mere diminutiveness.

STANDARD VARIETIES
Weights: Smooth-Haired dogs not to exceed 25 lb (11.3 kg); bitches not to exceed 23 lb (10.4 kg). Long-Haired dogs middle weight up to 18 lb (8.2 kg); Long-Haired dogs heavy weight over 18 lb (8.2 kg); bitches middle weight up to 17 lb (7.7 kg); heavy weight over 17 lb (7.7 kg). Wire-Haired dogs 20 – 22 lb (9 – 10 kg); bitches 18 – 20 lb (8.2 – 9 kg)
ALL MINIATURE VARIETIES
Weights: An ideal weight is 10 lb (4.5 kg).
Judges should not award a prize to any dog exceeding 11 lb (5 kg).

Deerhound

It is thought that, between the fifth and second centuries B.C., Celtic invaders brought with them to Scotland, dogs of the Greyhound type with rough coats which they used to hunt red stag, buck, deer, elk and wolf. Ancient rock carvings and cave paintings are to be found in Perthshire depicting this type of dog. It was so prized for its skill and ability in the chase that a battle is reported to have taken place between Scots and Picts in the year A.D. 277, during the reign of Cranthylinth, over the theft of one of these dogs. In A.D. 1016, King Canute decreed that only men of noble descent be allowed to keep a Deerhound in order to protect the deer of the royal forests from the depredations of commoners. In 1563, Mary Stuart, Queen of Scots, a keen huntress, brought back to her castle 360 stags and deer and five wolves, borne aloft in triumph to the sound o'horns and the skirl o'pipes by her retinue and followers.

However, by the end of the eighteenth century, the historian, Pennant, records that the Deerhound was becoming rare in the East of Scotland, due to the replacement of forest by cultivated land. In the nineteenth century, it was further threatened by the advent of the sporting-gun and the growing popularity of hunting on foot. But, thanks to Lord Colonsay and his brother Archibald McNeill, serious breeding began again in the 1820s and 50 years later, the breed was firmly re-established, although in smaller numbers. In 1891, the Scottish Deerhound Club was formed and the standard was drawn up in 1892. It appears in several chapters of Sir Walter Scott's novels and has an important place in the gallery of pictures by Sir Edwin Landseer, who painted it sitting gracefully at ease by a roaring fire, surveying the scene in the hall of the laird's highland castle after the day's hunting was finished.

As with the Irish Wolfhound, which it closely resembles in many ways and with which it was often confused before the nineteenth century, Deerhound-coursing has become popular among devotees. Dogs are led onto the field and liberated only when a hare is sighted, and then it is not so much catching the quarry that counts as gaining the highest number of points, according to the judge, for skill and ability in turning the hare as the dog covers the rough terrain with great leaping strides.

Considered as a show dog, it is one for the connoisseur and a parade of Deerhounds always attracts great attention. As with other big dogs, the breed was decimated during the two World Wars, but enthusiasts revived it afterwards and good entries are obtained at today's shows. Like the Irish Wolfhound, it is a natural dog and needs but little preparation for the ring. In character, it is impeccable, calm and obedient at all times and faithful to master and family, but it is of too friendly a nature to act as a guard dog and welcomes all visitors like long-lost friends. However, its sheer size acts as a deterrent. In common with other greyhound types, it is better kept indoors, where it can curl up small in its chosen place, but it must have access to an open space where it can work off stored-up energy; its movement in full flight is a joy to behold.

The head is broader at the ears, tapering to the eyes and throughout the

Ch Torffric Quilla, by Ch Finbar of Champflower, ex Ch Torffric Charlotte, brs Mrs & Mrs W. E. Jarrett, pr Mrs G. Smith

length of the muzzle to the nose. It is a long head with a rather flat skull and a slight rise over the eyes. The slightly aquiline nose is black, preferably, or blue. The skull is covered with fairly long, soft hair. It has a silky moustache and a fine beard. The eyes are dark brown or hazel, fairly full, with a soft look in repose and a far-away, keen look when roused; the rims are black. Ears are set on high and mobile, but not pricked, thick or flat. They are soft, glossy, small, dark in colour and with a silvery coat, but without fringe. The bite is level. The neck is fairly long and strong enough to hold a stag, and with a good mane in the adult. The nape is prominent and the throat clean-cut.

Forequarters have well-sloped shoulders with blades well back. The forelegs are broad and straight, with broad forearms and elbows. The body and formation is that of a big Greyhound. The chest is deep but not too narrow. The loin is well arched and drops to the tail. Hindquarters are drooping and as broad and powerful as possible, with hips set wide apart. Hindlegs are very long from hip to broad flat hocks and have well-bent stifles.

Feet are close and compact, with well-placed toes, good pads and strong nails. The tail is long, thick at the root and tapering to within 1½ in (3.8 cm) of the ground. It is curved when the dog is in motion but not above the line of the back. It has longer hair on the underside and sometimes a slight fringe at the end.

The coat has harsh wiry hair on the body, neck and quarters, about 3 or 4 in (7.6 or 10 cm) long; it is softer on the head, breast and belly. There is a slight fringe on the inside of the legs. The coat is thick, close-lying, harsh and ragged. As for colour, dark blue-grey is preferred, since quality tends to follow this colour. Next come darker and lighter greys and brindles, the darker being preferred. Yellow and sandy-red or red-fawn, especially with black points on ears and muzzle, are equally well liked, as they are the colours of the original McNeil strains. Touches of white on chest, toes and tip of tail are permissible, but are penalised elsewhere.

Height: dogs not less than 30in (76 cm); bitches not less than 28 in (71 cm).
Weight: dogs 85–105 lb (38.6–47.7 kg); bitches 65–80 lb (29.5–36.3 kg).

Elkhound

This hound, known in its own country as the Norsk Elghund-Grå is the national dog of Norway. Its conformation is that of the Spitz type seen throughout the Arctic and its principal function was to hunt in packs the formidable deer of those parts, the elk. A number of similar hounds were used in Scandinavia for this purpose, such as the Black Elkhound (Norsk Elghund-Sort), which is found largely in the Norwegian-Swedish border area and possesses a shorter coat, and the Swedish Elkhound (Jämthund), which is a taller and heavier dog of great strength. The last two, although recognised locally, like the Elkhound in 1877 when the Hunter's Association of Norway held its first show, are little known outside their own countries and are not recognised by the Kennel Club. Towards the end of the nineteenth century, the various kennel clubs of Scandinavia began to turn their attentions to improving the indigenous breeds and formulated a specification which they considered ideal for hunting; from then on breeders concentrated on achieving this type to the exclusion of others. The result was that the Elkhound as we know it today emerged and has gained great popularity since as a show dog, coming third after the Chow Chow and Samoyed in the Spitz breeds. It always attracts great attention in the ring, where it will stand perfectly still and quiet for the judge to inspect it; its beautiful movement is much praised as it strides round at an even and seemingly effortless trot with a perfectly level back and, as the speed increases, forelegs and hindlegs converge gradually towards a centre line under the body.

It is a lively dog of great courage and stamina — it needs to be in order to be able to hunt a gigantic elk through snow-covered forest-land, and hold it at bay until the huntsmen arrive to kill it; its keen scenting powers and virile resonant voice have proved it ideal for the job. It makes a good house dog and an excellent intelligent companion; it is free of odour and is especially fond of children; it can however at times show some independence of character.

Ch Ravenstone Hattie, by Hans Av Klekkefjell of Eskamere, ex Ravenstone Hiordis, brs Mr & Mrs Harper, pr Mr F. Pickup

The general appearance is that of the Spitz type, a prick-eared, compact dog with a fairly short body and with the tail curled over the back; like all similar dogs, it must have plenty of vigorous exercise if it is to keep in good form.

The head is wedge-shaped, broad between the ears with the forehead and the back of the head slightly arched. The stop is fairly small but clearly marked. The muzzle is moderately long, broader at the base and gradually tapering but not pointed; the bridge of the nose is straight and the jaw is strong with tight lips. Ears are erect, firm and set high, pointed and mobile; they are higher than their width at the base. Eyes are well set in, dark brown with a fearless but friendly expression. The mouth has strong teeth and a scissor bite. The neck is of medium length, well set up and firmly muscled.

Forequarters have elbows closely set on with firm, straight, powerful and well-boned legs with single dewclaws. The body is short in the couplings with a wide, deep, fairly broad chest and well-rounded ribs; the back is wide and straight and the loins are muscular. The belly is very little drawn up. Hindquarters have firm, strong hindlegs and a slight bend at stifle and hock;

the legs are straight viewed from the rear and without dewclaws.

Feet are compact and oval, pointing straight forward; toes are closed tightly and the nails are firm and strong. The tail is fairly short, set high and curled tightly over the back, but not on either side.

The coat is a distinctive feature of this hound. It is thick, abundant, coarse and weather-resistant, the ideal covering for working in intense cold over difficult terrain. Short on the head and the front of the legs, it is longest on the chest, neck, buttocks and behind the forelegs and on the underside of the tail. The topcoat is fairly long, coarse, and dark at the tips, with a light-coloured, soft woolly undercoat. In the region of the neck and front of chest, the coat forms a kind of ruff and this combines with the pricked ears, keen eyes and curled tail to give a rather special appearance. The only drawback is that the coat tends to shed drastically from time to time, with unfortunate results to the appearance of the dog and of any soft furnishings it comes in contact with. The various shades of grey with black tips are the colours of the top coat; the chest, legs, stomach and underside of the tail are of a lighter shade. Any variation from this grey colouring is undesirable, as are too dark or too light a shade.

Height: dogs 20½ in (52 cm); bitches 19½ in (49 cm).
Weight: dogs 50 lb (23 kg); bitches 43 lb (20 kg).
The American Kennel Club allows a weight up to 55 lb (25 kg) for dogs and 48 lb (21.8 kg) for bitches.

Finnish Spitz

Another of the Spitz family of dogs, but this time a 'bird dog', the Finnish Spitz' main job is to flush birds into trees, keeping them there until the arrival of the shooting party; it is also used for hunting small game. It is the national dog of Finland, where it is known as the Finsk Spets or Suomenpystykorva. It comes originally from the eastern part of Finland, where it has been known for hundreds of years. It is not surprising that the Russian Laïka, another bird-hunter from across the border, played a part in its development, in conjunction with other Spitz dogs of Scandinavia. It is referred to in the well-known Finnish saga *Kalevala* and, when Dr Axel Münthe, as a young man, spent a few weeks in Lapland, as he recalled later in his *Story of San Michele,* and slept in a smoke-filled tent with a Lapp family round the smouldering fire, a dog which could well have been very like this dog sidled slowly up to him:

> 'I felt in my sleep the warm weight of a dog over my breast and the soft touch of his nose in my hand.'

Ch Toveri Toby, by Ch Urkki of Toveri, ex Toveri Tippi, brs/prs Mrs Cavill, Mrs Minns & Mr Masters

The old Lapp, Turi, whose dog it was and who owned a thousand reindeer, was convinced that dogs had lost the power of speech when it was given to man, but they could understand every word you said to them.

This distinctive red variety of Spitz was recognised by the Finnish Kennel Club and the Fédération Cynologique Internationale, and a standard was drawn up towards the end of the nineteenth century. It very soon made an impression at dog shows. Lady Kitty Ritson was among the first to bring the breed to England in the early 1920s and gradually established a successful kennel from which many of today's dogs are descended. In more recent years, Mr and Mrs Dave and Angela Cavill's Toveri kennel, Mrs G. Price's Cullabine kennel and Miss P.A. McQuaide's Valpas kennel have produced some fine specimens of the breed and between them many superb champions. The Finnish Spitz Society keeps members well informed of progress at home and abroad in its quarterly newsletter.

The Finnish Spitz excels as regards temperament. It is intelligent, courageous and lively. Its keenness and good voice qualify it as a house dog; always on the alert, it is ready to guard family and property and its friendliness towards children is outstanding. Not the least of its virtues is the habit it shares with some other Spitz breeds of washing itself cat-fashion. Another unusual feature is that the male is considerably larger and has a much fuller coat than the female.

The head is foxy, of medium size with clean outlines; it is longer than it is broad in the ratio of 7:4. The forehead is slightly arched and the stop pronounced. Eyes are of medium size, almond-shaped and preferably dark; they have black rims, set slightly askant, with outer corners tilting upwards. The ears are small, cocked and sharply pointed; they are mobile and fine in texture. The muzzle is narrow and evenly tapering to the black nose. Lips are tight and thin and the bite is scissor. The neck is muscular and of medium length; the dense ruff found in the male makes it look shorter.

Forequarters are strong and straight and the body is almost square in outline, the height at the withers equalling the length of the body, with a strong straight back, deep chest and slightly drawn up belly. Hindquarters are strong with only a moderate turn of stifle.

The feet are perfectly round; hind dewclaws must be removed, but front dewclaws may remain. The tail is plumed, arching upward from the root, then forward, downward and backward, pressing down against the thigh, with its tip extending to the middle of it.

The coat is exceptionally beautiful. It is short and close on the head and the front of the legs, and longish and semi-erect or erect on the body and the back of the legs. It is stiffer on the back and on the neck where it forms a splendid ruff, especially in the male, whose outer coat is longer and coarser in the region of the shoulders. It is also longer and denser at the back of the thighs and on the tail. The undercoat is short, soft and dense. Trimming is not allowed. The colour is bright red-brown or red-gold on the back and of lighter shades in the ears, on the cheeks, under the muzzle, on the breast, on the abdomen, behind the shoulders, inside the legs, on the back of the thighs and the underside of the tail. The undercoat is also a lighter colour, making the whole coat glow. White markings on toes and a narrow white stripe on the breast are allowed. A few black points in the region of the lips, back and tail are desirable. The gait is light, springy, quick and graceful.

Height: dogs 17–20 in (44–50 cm); bitches 15½–18 in (39–45 cm).
Weight: dogs 31–36 lb (14–16 kg); bitches 23–29 lb (10–13 kg).

Foxhounds

The English Foxhound. The progenitors of the Foxhound are thought to be a number of Chiens Courants, which were presented, together with a few horses, by Henri IV of France to James I of England in 1603. Outcrossing with the Bloodhound and the Talbot had produced a good-looking hound which was very effective in hunting the fox. Huntsmen in Britain adapted and developed them to suit their own purposes, sometimes adding

Goodwill, from the Duke of Beaufort's strain, Ashford Valley Hunt

Greyhound blood where increased speed was needed and Welsh Foxhound blood for more stamina; the records and stud books kept by the various hunts over the centuries make very interesting reading.

The Foxhound as we know it is never seen at dog shows as no classes are provided by the Kennel Club, although there must be several thousand in England alone, but it takes part instead at meets and gatherings organised by the Masters of Foxhounds Association which, rather than the Kennel Club, is the authority responsible for this breed; some, however, are shown on the Continent. Puppies are looked after by the hunt supporters, who act as puppy-walkers in a similar way to those families who care for young dogs destined to become guide dogs for the blind. When they are old enough, meets are arranged and the puppies put on show for all to see and assess, a very colourful event in a convivial atmosphere. An adult Foxhound, however, is not suitable as a house dog or pet, needing as they do a vast amount of vigorous exercise, preferably with horses and in groups. They are fed mostly on horse meat, flaked maize and mashed oatmeal from trenchers, the weaker hounds being let in to eat first; they are never fed during the 24 hours previous to hunting. The Foxhound has appeared in many pictures by English artists such as Landseer, Mullins and Baxter, and some of the best hunt-scenes are to be seen in sequences in Eric Porter's film *The Belstone Fox*, the touching story of an orphaned fox cub brought up by a hound bitch with her own puppies and the dire consequences which ensued for all concerned.

Although the type varies to some extent, as hunting suitability takes precedence over appearance, an overall symmetry is looked for. The head and skull are typically broad and the neck is long without being thick. A short-necked hound is deficient in pace. Forequarters have shoulders that show quality and no lumber. Too fleshy a shoulder prevents the hound running at top speed up and down hill. Elbows are set straight. Legs are well boned right down, straight, strong and do not taper off; they have good ankle bone. The body is deep with plenty of heart and lung room; the back is broad and well ribbed up and there should be a fair space between the end of the ribs and the hindquarters to ensure a good stride. Hindquarters are full and very muscular. Stifles are straight and hocks well let down. The hindlegs are well boned throughout and straight like the forelegs. The feet are round and the toes close together with good knuckles. The tail is well set on, carried gaily, and tapers to a point. The coat is short, dense and hard in texture and of the usual hound colours, i.e. combinations of black, tan and white.

Height: dogs 23 in (58.5 cm); bitches 22 in (56 cm).
Weight: relative to height.

The Welsh Foxhound. This hound is indigenous to Wales and is never seen outside the Principality. Although of similar general appearance to the English Foxhound, it has a distinguishing feature in its rough-haired coat, an unusual characteristic in hounds of this type. Some historians think it is descended from the ancient Celtic hound from which evolved a type of Welsh Hound. Certain crossings are said to have taken place with French hounds brought as gifts from Brittany and Normandy by monks in the tenth and eleventh centuries to the Abbey of Margram in South-West Wales; some Fell Hound and English Foxhound blood was probably added at a later date. At first used for deer-hunting, it became more and more a fox-hunter as sheep-farmers became more numerous and required it to keep down the fox population. Some enthusiasts have regretted the introduction of Fell Hound and Foxhound blood as being somewhat detrimental to its keenness of scent, to its distinctive bay and to its powers of propulsion. When Henry VIII closed the abbeys, Margram was taken over by the members of the Welsh aristocracy, who kept on the kennels until the nineteenth century when they were finally disbanded. Parson Jack Russell, of terrier fame, managed to acquire a few of the hounds and, with Elwyn Llewellyn, an old friend, succeeded in perpetuating the breed and restoring the old type which was more suitable for mountainous country. It is used like the English Foxhound, and also with the gun. When the hunting season is over, the packs are usually dispersed, the dogs being kept by followers until next season. Like the English Foxhound, it is shown only at gatherings organised by the Welsh Foxhound Association which keeps the stud book.

Medoc, from the New Forest Hunt

The head is fairly long, the stop being halfway between the occiput and the nose. The ears are set low, below eye level, and their tips can reach the nose when pulled forward. The scent and bay are particularly good in today's dog and very valuable in the terrain it works and where it often outdistances the field. Although its general conformation is very similar to that of the English Foxhound, its coat is rough and hard of texture and of much lighter colour, mostly white with faded lemon markings on ears and back, other hound colours being less common.

Height: dogs 24 in (61 cm); bitches 21 in (53 cm).
Weight: relative to height.

41

The American Foxhound. This hound differs from the English and Welsh varieties in that it is a show dog as well as a working dog and is often seen at shows throughout the States, but does not have championship status in Great Britain. The first pack was founded in Maryland in the middle of the seventeenth century by Robert Brooke, who brought his hounds from England; his family, all keen huntsmen, have carried on the kennels ever since. In the 1770s, President Washington imported more English

Ch American Foxhound; details unknown

Foxhounds and, about 10 years later, was presented by Lafayette with some French hounds which he crossed with them, resulting in the famous Virginia strain. The original stock was given new blood from time to time by imported dogs from England, France and Ireland, and a number of hounds of choice English stock were also imported by the Gloucester (U.S.A.) Foxhunting Club at the beginning of the nineteenth century. Several different types emerged until the American Kennel Club drew up a standard for show purposes in 1894. The types vary somewhat according to the work which they do; some are used to work with the gun, like the Welsh Foxhound, others take part at Field Trial events, and others at Drag meets, like the Fellhounds of the Lake District. The standard dog, however, does the work of the English Foxhound and hunts in the pack, running the fast American red fox to ground in traditional manner.

The American Foxhound is rather more imposing than its English cousin. It is longer in the leg and stands a little taller and has a more racy outline, being lighter in weight. The head is long and slightly domed, with a broad skull. The ears are set fairly low and do not quite reach the tip of the nose when pulled forward; they are round at the tip and fine in texture. The eyes are large, set well apart, brown or hazel in colour. The stop is moderate and the muzzle fairly long, straight and square-cut. The neck is strong and of medium length. Forequarters have sloping shoulders and the chest is deep and narrower in relation to depth than that of the English Foxhound. Forelegs are straight with good bone and short straight pasterns. Feet are foxy, with full hard pads and well-arched toes. The ribs are well sprung, the back fairly long and muscular and the loins broad and slightly arched. Hips and thighs are well muscled with great powers of propulsion. Stifles are well let down and hocks moderately bent. Feet are close and firm. The tail is long and set fairly high, with a slight curve and coarse hair on the underside. The coat is close and hard and of medium length; it can be of any hound colour.

Height: dogs 22–25 in (56–63 cm); bitches 21–24 in (53–61 cm).
Weight: relative to height.

Greyhound

The history of the Greyhound goes back to most ancient times; we find it depicted in Assyrian and Egyptian monuments of the region of the Nile in the period around 4,000 B.C. and in the Tunis mosaics. The Eastern sighthound found its way to Europe, passing through Greece and the Roman colonies of North Africa. It traversed Italy and France in the Middle Ages and was brought to the shores of England by the Celts. In Saxon times, only nobles were permitted by decree to keep it, as in the case of the Deerhound, in order to protect royal game from the poorer classes; the killing of a hound was a heinous crime, punishable by death. In the sixteenth century, it was used for buck-coursing in Britain. All chroniclers have stressed the fantastic vision, superb hearing, speed and grace of this beautiful hound, which was often given to a lady as a token of love. Its proverbial faithfulness to its master is exemplified in the story of the Duke of Enghien who, when he was seized during the night of the 15th–16th March 1804, by agents of Napoleon, was followed by his favourite Greyhound. Beaten off by hostile clubs as it tried to get into the boat taking its master away across the fast-flowing river, the dog swam over to the other side. Only then was the Duke allowed to have it and the dog remained with him until his death by firing squad in the woods of Vincennes. The Duke was buried on the spot where he fell and the dog kept watch over his grave until several days later, when it too died of hunger and grief. A Greyhound is sometimes carved on a nobleman's tomb as a sign of fidelity.

Ch Shalfleet Stormlight, by Am Ch Aroi Sea Hawk of Shalfleet, ex Ch Shalfleet Spotlight, br/pr Mrs B. Wilton-Clark

The Saxon word *greu* means 'dog of high degree' and, indeed, the Greyhound's breeding is so pure that its conformation has varied hardly at all during 7,000 years. It is the subject of many beautiful paintings by seventeenth-century Dutch painters and, of course, by Landseer. Prince Albert of Saxe-Cobourg was given a birthday present of a beautiful black-and-white Greyhound called Eos, which he brought to England when he married Queen Victoria. He hunted with it in the Windsor parks and forests and had specially made for it a solid silver collar, engraved and pierced, and equipped with a lock which had an ingenious combination. Landseer was commissioned by the Queen to paint it as a surprise Christmas present for the Duke; the portrait shows Eos in profile with jet-black glossy coat and white blaze, star and feet.

The days when this hound was hunted have now passed and, as a sporting dog, it is used today only in coursing and on the race track, a sport first started in America and which is now world-wide, with top honours going to Irish-bred dogs, such as the champion of champions, Mick the Miller, the greatest racing Greyhound of all, now preserved in the British Museum (Natural History). Although the Whippet has the faster take-off speed, the Greyhound can usually reach 50 mph (80 km/h) on the straight. Its temperament is superb, as is usual with the sighthounds; it makes an excellent sporting companion and dogs retired from the track make good

44

pets. The Greyhound can do 250 m in less than 15 seconds. Over a distance of 480 m, it holds the record of 29.57 seconds for a sighthound.

As a show dog, it is quite popular and, for this purpose, a dog of slightly greater stature is preferred. The Greyhound is of the basic *graioïde* type, according to the morphological typology of Megnin. It is a strongly-built, upstanding dog of generous proportions, muscular power and symmetrical formation, great stamina and endurance and straight-through, long-reaching free movement, with hindlegs coming well under the body to give great propulsion.

The head is long, of moderate width with a flat skull and slight stop. Jaws are powerful and well chiselled. The eyes are bright, oval and set obliquely, and ears are small, rose-shaped and of fine texture. The teeth are strong and the bite scissor. The neck is long, muscular and elegantly arched.

Forequarters have oblique, well-laid shoulders, clearly defined at the top. Forelegs are long and straight with good bone. Elbows are free and well set under the shoulders, and pasterns are of moderate length and slightly sprung, both pointing straight forward. The chest is deep, giving good heart and lung room. Ribs are well sprung and carried well back; the flanks are well tucked up and the back long and broad. The loin is slightly arched. Hindquarters have wide muscular thighs and second thighs with great propelling power. Stifles are well bent and hocks well let down, again pointing straight forward. Body and hindquarters are of ample proportions and well coupled, covering plenty of ground.

The feet are fairly long with compact, well-knuckled toes, pointing forward and strongly padded. The tail is long and set on rather low, strong at the root, tapering to a point, slightly curved and carried low. The coat is fine and close, and the colours are white, black, red, blue, fawn, fallow, brindle or any of these colours with white markings.

Height: dogs 28 – 30 in (71 – 76 cm); bitches 27 – 28 in (68 – 71 cm).
Weight: relative to height.

Hamiltonstövare

Count Hamilton of Sweden, who is responsible for the creation and development of this beautiful hound, the youngest of the three stövare (hounds) of that country, was also the founder of the Swedish Kennel Club towards the end of the nineteenth century. Around the middle of the century, he had started a breeding programme, taking local hounds as his point of departure and adding, by successive outcrossing, the blood of the English Foxhound and various German hounds, such as the Holsteinerhund and the

Acke of Barclan, by Swed Sh & F Tr Ch Liljansvallens Stoj II, ex Luldalens Bella II, br Mr H. Lundmark, pr Mrs B. J. Stewart   David Dalton

Heidebracke from Hanover, both now extinct. It is thought that the Courlander and the Swiss Laufhund also played a part in his experiments. At the Stockholm Dog Show in 1886, the first show to be held in Sweden, there were over a hundred Hamiltonstövare entered. What is certain is that the Hamiltonstövare is now the most popular of all Swedish hounds, not only in Sweden but also abroad where its calm bearing and striking appearance as a show dog is much appreciated. It was first imported into Great Britain in 1968.

It was however as a worker and hunter that the Count had bred it, to hunt, not like the Foxhound in the pack, but singly or in couples as gun dogs to flush game in the forests for the following huntsmen to shoot. Neither are these dogs kept in group kennels but in the home as friendly family pets. The Hamiltonstövare has a very good nose and a pleasant sounding bay and will hunt tirelessly all day in the deep snow of its native country. It is a handsome, tall, strong dog, full of stamina, and well proportioned. Although somewhat independent of character, it is quite intelligent and easy to handle in the show ring, where its bright, elegant, tri-coloured coat shows up well.

The head is fairly long and rectangular with a slightly arched, moderately broad skull. The occiput is not too prominent and the stop is well defined.

The muzzle is fairly long, large and more pointed than in other stövare; the bridge is straight and parallel to the top of the skull. The nose is black with large nostrils and the upper lips are full but not overhanging. The eyes are dark brown and clear and the ears are flat, of moderate length and hanging close to the head. The jaws and teeth are strong with scissor bite, the upper incisors closely overlapping the lower. The long powerful neck merges well into the shoulders and has a supple close-fitting skin.

Forequarters have muscular well-laid-back shoulders. The upper forelegs are long and broad and set at right angles to the shoulder blades. The elbows are set closely in to the body. Viewed from the front, the forelegs are straight and parallel. The back is level and strong. The croup is long, broad and slightly inclined with well-defined muscles. The chest is deep and the ribs moderately sprung with proportionally long back ribs. The belly is slightly tucked up. The hindquarters are muscular and broad, well angulated when seen from the side and parallel viewed from behind.

The feet are short and hard, with firm pads, and point straight forward. Dewclaws are removed. The gait is free-striding with a long-reaching high action; the hindlegs have a powerful drive and should not move close behind. The tail is set on high, continuing the line of the back. It is held straight or slightly curving in a sabre-like fashion when the dog is in action. Fairly wide at the base, it narrows towards the tip and stretches to the hock.

The coat is double, having a weather-resistant topcoat, lying close to the body, and a soft, short, close undercoat, which grows very thick in the winter. The hair is fairly long on the underside of the tail, but does not form a fringe. The coloration is an outstanding feature of this hound. It is tri-coloured: black on the upperside of the neck, the back, the sides of the trunk and the upperside of the tail; brown on the head and legs, the side of the neck, the rest of the trunk and the underside of the tail. It should have a white blaze, white on the lower neck and breast, and white feet and tip of tail. The three colours should be definite, clearly separated and in even proportions.

Height: dogs 19½–23½ in (50–60 cm); bitches 18–22½ in (46–57 cm).
Weight: relative to height.

Ibizan Hound

The Ibizan Hound comes from the Island of Ibiza off the East coast of Spain, where it is known as the Podenco Ibicenco. It is also to be found in smaller numbers on Mallorca, Menorca and the small island of Formentera. It has been known for centuries in a form almost identical to its present conformation and has been used in the islands and on the Spanish mainland

47

*Ch Paran Prima Donna, by Papyrus of Ivicen, ex Ch Divels Nana, br Mrs
Stoneham, prs Mr & Mrs Stoneham*

for hare- and rabbit-coursing and for deer-hunting in Andalucia and on the
Catalonian coast. It is closely related to the Pharaoh Hound and the
Portuguese Podengo and, like them, can claim to have had ancestors living in
the times of the ancient Egyptians some 3,000 years B.C., on whose
monuments and papyri can be seen depicted hounds of strikingly similar
conformation and vari-coloration with the pricked ears which distinguish it
from other sighthounds, such as the Sloughi and Saluki, which are also to be
found painted there. Archaeologists have unearthed bones of similar hounds
dating back a further 2,000 years! It is possible that traders took hounds with
them to various Mediterranean ports and that some found their way to the
Spanish Islands. We know that, when the Romans invaded Egypt, the
Carthaginians and Phoenicians in neighbouring territories fled to Spain in
800–900 B.C., again bringing similar dogs, which have remained there to
this day.

Although the Ibizan Hound is definitely a sighthound in conformation, it
has a good nose and hunts also by scent. Only the ears show a blood of
different origin, probably from the same source as that of the Basenji. The
Smooth-Coated hound is the one most favoured, although Wire- and Long-
Haired examples are present. It is an excellent hunter of small game,
especially hare and rabbits, and has the curious habit of jumping up almost
vertically to over 6 ft (1.8 m) without a take-off run to have a good look round

48

for game, and not only will it be sure to catch it but also to retrieve it to hand. A couple can account for hundreds of hares and rabbits in a few hours. It normally works by day, but it is equally good at night with the lamp. It is also useful as a gun dog.

Its temperament is superb and it makes a good house dog, being calm and affectionate with everyone it knows, especially with young people and children, but it is a little cautious with strangers. It avoids fighting with other dogs at all costs; this is not because of lack of spirit but possibly because it strongly dislikes too much noise, its powers of hearing being so sharp that its sensitive nature is intensified; indeed when it needs correcting a quiet word of warning is all that is necessary, anything more would be too severe. Its commanding presence has made it a popular modern show dog, needing only a little preparation for the ring; the smooth variety is the most popular for show purposes. It was first imported into the United States in 1956 and was recognised by the American Kennel Club in 1979. It is a tireless, controlled hunter with great stamina and style.

The head is finely sculptured and well balanced, with a long, flat skull and prominent occipital bone. The stop is moderate and the muzzle slightly convex, the distance from eye to nose equalling that from eye to occiput. The nose is flesh-coloured and protrudes beyond the incisors. The jaw is strong and lean. The eyes are clear amber, almond-shaped, expressive and of medium size. Ears are large, thin, stiff and mobile; they are erect when the dog is alert. When viewed in profile, they are in a continuous line with the arch of the neck; the base is set on level with the eyes. The mouth has even white teeth and a scissor bite with thin lips and no dewlap. The neck is lean, long, muscular, and slightly arched.

Forequarters have rather steep, short shoulder blades, long, straight legs and erect pasterns. The back is level, sloping only slightly from pinbones to rump. The rib cage is long and flat. The dog is short-coupled with well-tucked-up waist and very prominent breastbone. Hindquarters are long, strong, straight and lean, without great angulation. The second thigh is long.

The feet have well-arched toes, thick pads and light-coloured nails. Front feet may turn slightly outwards. The tail is long, thin, low set and reaches well below the hock; it may be carried high when the dog is alert, but not curled or low over the back.

The coat is smooth or rough; it is hard, close and dense, longer under the tail and behind the legs. The colours are white, chestnut or lion-coloured, or any combination of these. The gait is a suspended trot, a long far-reaching stride, with a slight hover before placing the foot to the ground.

Height: 22–29 in (56–74 cm).
Bitches are usually smaller than dogs, balance being the overriding factor.
Weight: relative to height.

Irish Wolfhound

Irish legend tells of the great wolfdogs of the Emerald Isle, 'the dogs that Fingal bred', such as Brann who, it appears, had supernatural powers and belonged to the worthy chieftain Finn, whilst others performed innumerable deeds of courage and great endurance. King John of England gave such a dog, called Gelert, to his son Llewellyn, Prince of Wales, in 1210. The Prince left his baby son Owain in the charge of Gelert and went off to the hunt. When he returned he could not see the boy in the mist which had fallen and, finding only Gelert with blood dripping from his jaws, he flew into a rage and ran the dog through with his sword. Too late, he turned round and caught sight of the boy and lying near him the huge wolf that the faithful Gelert had fought and killed in his defence!

Ch Seplecur Meg of Sulhamstead, by Ch Sulhamstead Motto, ex Ch Seplecur Meghan, br Mrs G. A. Crane, prs Mrs F. Nagle & Miss M. G. Ellis

Going back still further to the fourth century, Irish wolfdogs are reported to have taken part in combats in Roman arenas, where they were described as *canes scotici*. Reinagle said, in his *Sportsman's Cabinet* in 1804, that they were 'larger than the Mastiff, exceedingly ferocious when engaged'. An image of the dog appears on the insignia of ancient Irish Kings, who used it in battle as well as for the hunt. But, by the eighteenth century, there were few wolves left in Ireland and the huge dog was relegated to become the companion of nobility and to accompany them in the chase of the elk, a rôle in which it proved to be very effective. It was, according to Oliver Goldsmith, who wrote of it in his book *Animated Nature* in 1796, 'extremely beautiful and majestic as to appearance, being the greatest of the dog kind to be seen in the world'.

The breed declined in the years that followed until halfway through the nineteenth century, when a number of enthusiasts set about resurrecting it, among them Sir John Power of Kilfane, who, with the Scottish Captain G.A. Graham at his kennels in England, is responsible for the dogs we have today. The original Irish strains were infused with Scottish Deerhound, Great Dane and Borzoi blood to produce a tall, graceful, commanding hound of prestigious proportions. Captain Graham formed the Irish Wolfhound Club in 1885 and a standard was drawn up; the English Kennel Club recognised the breed in 1897. Although World War 1 caused breeding programmes to be drastically curtailed, the Irish Wolfhound Coursing Club was formed in 1924 in Britain for the purpose of coursing hare and, later, in the United States, when lure-coursing gained popularity, the use of live game being proscribed in that country, many enthusiasts found great sport in pitting their hounds against each other after the lure.

The Irish Wolfhound is now seen at shows throughout the world where it never fails to attract a great deal of attention as it stands imperiously in the ring. Although not so heavy or massive as the Great Dane, it is taller and very graceful with an easy movement, carrying its head high and its tail in an upward sweep, with a slight curve towards the end. It is keen of sight and fleet of foot and in temperament it is faultless, noble in every way, gentle with the smallest child, yet with an appearance and resonant voice capable of deterring the most desperate of miscreants.

The head is long with the frontal bones of the forehead very slightly raised and only slight indentation between the eyes. The skull is not too broad and the muzzle is long and moderately tapering. The eyes are dark brown and the ears small and rose-shaped. Jaws and teeth are very strong with level bite; lips and nose are black. The neck is very strong and muscular, of good length and well arched. There is no dewlap or loose skin on the throat.

Forequarters have muscular, clean, sloping shoulders, providing a proud head carriage and correct balance between the neck and back. Elbows are set well under and held close to the side. The forelegs and forearms are muscular, well boned, straight and strong. The chest is broad and very deep and the back moderately long. The loins are arched and the belly well drawn up. The body is long, well ribbed up, with well-sprung ribs and great breadth across the hips. Hindquarters are long and strong with muscular, well-boned thighs and long, strong second thighs. Stifles are nicely bent and hocks are well let down and parallel.

Feet are round and fairly large, pointing straight forward. Toes are well arched and compact, with very strong curved nails. The tail is long, slightly curved, fairly thick and well covered with hair.

The coat is rough, hard and of moderate length on the body, head and legs; it is especially wiry and long over the eyes and under the jaw. The colours are light or dark grey, blue-grey, brindle, red, black, pure white, fawn, or yellow, with or without black points.

Height: dogs 31 in (79 cm); bitches 28 in (71 cm).
Weight: dogs 120 lb (54.5 kg); bitches 90 lb (40.9 kg).
These are minimum requirements for height and weight of dogs over 18 months old. Great size is to be aimed at with an average height of 32–34 in (81–86 cm) for dogs, which must have the requisite power, activity, courage and symmetry.

Otterhound

The Otterhound is a very old British breed dating back to the time of King John, who owned the first pack at the beginning of the thirteenth century; it is, in fact, referred to in even earlier documents. There seems to be no doubt that the old Southern Hound, the Saint-Hubert and the French Griffons (Vendéen, Nivernais, Fauves de Bretagne and de Bresse) played an important part in its make-up; indeed, in many points of conformation, it closely resembles the Bloodhound and enjoys similar keenness of scent, being able to find and successfully follow a trail in water. Not only King John, but also Henry II and Elizabeth I and a number of monasteries, maintained large packs of Otterhounds to keep down the otter population, which was a constant threat to fish stock in the rivers and private storage ponds. In the following years, it seems that outcrossing took place, in order to preserve and improve stamina, with the Harrier, Staghound, Foxhound and Kerry Beagle.

An excellent swimmer, being endowed with large, wide-spreading, webbed feet, it is ideal for otter-hunting. The type was standardised in the nineteenth century, when there were twenty-five or so packs in England and Wales. The numbers of otters gradually decreased, however, to the point where extinction appeared to be not far off and, therefore, the sport of otter-hunting was eventually banned. To preserve the Otterhound in its turn from dying out, now that its purpose no longer existed, the Master of the Kendal and District Otterhounds pack, just before its dispersal, decided to form the Otterhound Club of Great Britain. A nucleus of enthusiastic breeders in Cumbria and elsewhere still keep the flag flying, and the breed, although classified now as a rare breed, makes sporadic appearances at championship shows. It was exported to the United States of America at the turn of the

Dumfriesshire Cypher at Trevereux, by Dumfriesshire Bargeman, ex Dumfriesshire Traceable, br Capt J. Bell-Irving, pr Mrs J. Wiginton

century and has enjoyed some popularity there.

Although it makes a good guard dog, it is hardly suitable as a family pet due to its size and shaggy waterproof coat; it is a very friendly animal, especially towards children, and has a calm even temperament and amiable disposition. It is a big, well-built, rough-coated hound with a majestic head and free long-striding action, and its swimming skill rivals that of the Newfoundland.

The head is deep and rather wide, with good cheek bones and a domed skull with slight occipital peak and distinct stop. The muzzle is strong and deep with a good nose, wide nostrils and plenty of lip and flew. Distance from nose tip to stop is slightly shorter than from stop to occiput. Eyes are fairly deep set with the haw showing slightly. The colour of the eyes and rims varies according to the shade of the coat. Ears are long and pendulous, having a characteristic single fold, the leading edge rolling inwards. The mouth is strong, large, preferably with scissor bite, but level bite is permissible. The neck is moderately long and powerful set into well-laid-back shoulders. A slight dewlap is permissible.

Forequarters have strongly boned forelegs, which are straight from elbows to ground. Pasterns are strong and slightly sprung. The chest is deep with a well-sprung, fairly long, oval rib cage, and ribs carried well back, allowing plenty of room for heart and lungs. The back is broad with level topline. The loin is short and strong. Hindquarters are very strong and well muscled, with fairly well-bent stifle and well-let-down hocks; thighs and second thighs are heavily muscled.

The feet are large, round, well knuckled, thickly padded and pointing forward. They are compact when standing, but webbed and capable of spreading. The tail is set high and carried up, straight or in a slight curve, when the dog is on the move, but not over the back; it may droop when standing. It is thick at the base, tapering to a point, the bone reaching to the hock.

The top coat is about 1½−3 in (4−8 cm) long, dense and harsh, with a waterproof undercoat, both having a slightly oily texture. It is a natural hound, requiring no trimming. The head is well covered with rough hair, with slight whiskers and beard and a ruff round the neck. The hair on the underside of the tail is longer than the hair on the topside. The colour is generally sandy, fawn or shaded grey with black-and-tan markings, but any of the recognised hound colours are permissible, with or without slight white markings on head, chest, feet and tail tip. Pigmentation should harmonise with coat colour, but a slight butterfly nose is allowed.

The peculiar gait is loose and shambling when walking, but springing into a loose, sound, active trot; the gallop is smooth and very long-striding.

The Otterhound is happily to be seen again in the show ring and the Otterhound Club is holding its own shows. The first of these was judged by Captain John Bell-Irving, Joint Master of the Dumfriesshire Otterhounds, which still hunt coypu and mink in Scotland since otter-hunting was proscribed in January, 1978. The Best in Show award at the first three shows went to that excellent dog Dumfriesshire Cypher at Trevereux, bred in the Dumfriesshire pack and now owned by Mrs Janet Wiginton.

Height: dogs 27 in (67 cm); bitches 24 in (61 cm).
Weight: relative to height.

Pharaoh Hound

This hound is closely related to the Ibizan Hound, sharing to a high degree its origin, history and evolution. Drawings and reliefs found on the walls of ancient tombs show prick-eared, Pharaoh-type hounds as canine personifications of the Egyptian God of the Jackal, Anubis. The Fédération Cynologique Internationale recognises the Ibizan Hound and the Pharaoh Hound as separate breeds, as do the Kennel Club and the American Kennel Club, although many have considered the latter to be a coloured variety of the former. It is quite probable that the Pharaoh Hound was brought to Malta

Ch Furnwood Argus, by Ch Merymut Sahure, ex Merymut Cassiopeia, brs Mr & Mrs Welsh, pr Mrs V. White

and Gozo by the Phoenician merchants at the same time as the Ibizan Hound was brought from Egypt to the Spanish islands and the Cirneco dell'Etna to Sicily, the latter being little known outside its own island. Indeed, the Pharaoh Hound too was hardly seen outside Malta, where it has been known for over 2,000 years, until the early 1970s, but its popularity grew so rapidly that it was given championship status in 1975.

Dr George Reisner, of the Harvard-Boston archaeological expedition, in 1935, in a cemetery near the Pyramid of Cheops at Giza, found a record of the ceremonial burial of Abuwtiyuw, a dog of this type; it was so highly thought of that it had been allotted a tomb to itself. The present-day dog has been bred to type on the Island of Malta for thousands of years, where it is still prized as a skilled rabbit-catcher. Like the Ibizan Hound, it uses both sight and scent when hunting, and it shares its even temperament and tractability in the show ring, well-attended classes being put on for it at many of the big shows. Its beautiful, short, glossy, predominantly red or tan coat is one of its most attractive points and accounts for much of its rise to fame as a show dog. It poses and moves well in the ring and never seeks to quarrel with its peers. There is no doubt that this dog, although late on the scene, has a great future as a show specimen. Cautious with strangers, it is very affectionate with its owner and family and needs very little attention to keep it in first class shape; one of its great delights is playing with children whom it adores. It is a graceful, powerful dog of noble bearing and makes an excellent watch and guard dog.

The head is wedge-shaped. The skull is long, lean and well chiselled, with the foreface slightly longer than the skull, the top of skull and foreface being parallel. There is a slight stop. The eyes are amber in colour and blend with the coat. They are oval and moderately deep set with a keen intelligent expression. Ears are medium high set, broad at the base, fine and large; they are mobile and carried erect when alert. The jaws are powerful with strong teeth and scissor bite. The nose is flesh-coloured, blending with the coat. The neck is long, lean, muscular and slightly arched with a clean throat line.

Forequarters have strong, well-laid-back shoulders. The forelegs are straight and parallel, with elbows well tucked in and strong pasterns. The body is lithe with an almost straight topline. There is a slight slope down from croup to root of tail. The deep brisket extends down to point of elbow. The ribs are well sprung with a moderate cut up. The length of the body from breast to haunch bone is slightly longer than the height at the withers. Hindquarters are strong and muscular with moderate bend of stifle and a well-developed second thigh. The legs are parallel viewed from behind.

The feet are strong, well knuckled and pointing forward. Paws are well padded. The tail is medium set, thick at the base and tapering to reach to just below the point of the hock. It is curved and carried high in action.

The coat is short and glossy, ranging from fine and close to slightly harsh, and without feathering. The colour is reddish, tan or rich tan with white markings on tip of tail and toes, and with a white star on the chest and a slim white blaze. Flecking or white markings other than those mentioned are undesirable in Britain but are seen on the Continent.

The gait is free and flowing, with the head held fairly high and the dog covering the ground effortlessly, legs and feet moving in line with the body.

Height: dogs 22 – 25 in (56 – 63 cm); bitches 21 – 24 in (53 – 61 cm).
Overall balance is the overriding factor, weight being relative to height.

Rhodesian Ridgeback

The courage of the Rhodesian Ridgeback is such that it is not deterred by the most formidable of game and has been known to give a good account of itself against the leopard in its native country. Its progenitors were the lion-hunting hounds of the Hottentot tribe of South Africa, who had brought it in the first place from Asia and who valued their ridgebacked dogs equally with their humpbacked cattle. There is no doubt that this hound was crossed with hounds brought in subsequently by early white settlers in the sixteenth and

Ch Rejan Mandingo, by Mac of Resan, ex Rejan Super Girl, br/pr Mr J. Parker

seventeenth centuries from Europe; these people, mostly consisting of Dutch, Germans and Huguenots, brought with them their various kinds of running dogs, and perhaps the Great Dane (*Deutsche Dogge*) to which it bears some resemblance, and crossed them with the lion dogs. These outcrosses refined and matured it considerably as far as temperament was concerned, but without depriving it of its distinctive mark, the ridge along the spine. This ridge is formed by hair growing in the reverse direction to the rest of the coat along the back; it looks like a sword with two crowns near the shoulders and the point at the hip bones. It is the only dog to possess this unique mark.

A missionary from South Africa is said to have brought a couple to Rhodesia, where they were used with great success on big game safaris. In Livingstone's *Missionary Travels in South Africa*, published in 1857, we find a picture of an early Ridgeback. The big-game-hunter, Cornelius van Ruyen, played a leading part in its development. On safari, it is used to chase and hold the lion at bay for the hunters to shoot rather than to engage it in combat itself; this is where its great speed, strength and agility prove to be so valuable. It is also used against smaller quarry and it contents itself on these occasions by simply knocking them down. It is now the national dog of South Africa and has been a firm favourite at dog shows there since the 1920s, when a breed club was formed, a standard drawn up and careful breeding programmes initiated.

It makes an excellent companion for children and a superb guard for home, person and property; although the ferocity of its ancestors has been completely bred out, making it one of the quietest and best to handle in the show ring, it can make known its displeasure by a deep threatening growl and a look in the eye which is always enough to dissuade any intruder. Rather indolent in demeanour and, like some of the Greyhound types, quite happy to lie around for hours on end, it can undergo a rapid transformation when game is sighted and it is then that its speed and beauty are seen at their best, with a straight forward, free-moving gait similar to that of the Foxhound.

The head is fairly long, with a flat skull, rather broad between the ears and free from wrinkle when in repose. The stop is fairly well defined. The nose is black in red-wheaten dogs and brown in light-wheaten ones. Dark eyes go with a black nose and amber eyes with a brown nose. Eyes are set well apart and are round with a keen expression. Ears are set rather high and of medium size and tapering to a rounded point; they are carried close to the head. The muzzle is long, deep and powerful, the jaws level and strong with well-developed teeth, especially the canines. The lips closely fit the jaws. The neck is fairly long, strong and free from throatiness.

Forequarters have sloping muscular shoulders which denote speed, elbows close to the body, and straight, heavily boned legs. The chest is not too wide but very deep, giving plenty of heart and lung room; the ribs are moderately well sprung. The back is powerful with strong, slightly arched loins. Hindquarters have legs with well-defined musculature and the hocks are well let down.

The feet are compact with well-arched toes with hair between them for protection, and have round tough pads. The tail has a medium setting, is strong and tapers to the end; it is carried with a slight upward curve and must not curl.

The coat is short and dense, sleek and glossy; it must not be woolly or silky. The colour is light-wheaten to red-wheaten, with head, body and legs of the same colour and a small white star on the chest. Ears and muzzle can be dark.

Height: dogs 25−27 in (63−68 cm); bitches 24−26 in (61−66 cm).
Weight: dogs 75−85 lb (34.1−38.5 kg); bitches 65−75 lb (29.5−33.9 kg).

58

Saluki

The Saluki, Gazelle Hound or Persian Greyhound, as it is variously called, has much in common with the Afghan Hound and the Sloughi, not least in origin, as all three stem from the ancient Middle Eastern Greyhound. As in their cases, there are dogs pictured in the old cave paintings which have the characteristic featherings of the Saluki, the type which has evolved as the dog of the Bedouin tribesman, taking its name from the Saluk in the Yemen. Carvings and paintings dating back to 6,000 B.C. show a Saluki-type hound running beside its master, who is riding after gazelle or similar quarry. The method of hunting was, as with the Afghan Hound, to hunt with horse, falcon and dogs, the falcon being released when the quarry was sighted in order to attack its head and allow the dogs to catch up and drag it down. The tombs of the Pharaohs also show similar scenes of the hunt, with hounds of like conformation. Little has changed since those far-off times and life and customs in the desert have remained constant. Like its cousins, the Saluki is revered by the tribesmen and jealously guarded, since, of course, it is instrumental in providing fresh meat in inhospitable surroundings and so earns the respect that it is accorded. Gazelle, hare and jackal all fall before the speed, strength and endurance of this great-hearted hound, in sure-footed pursuit, whether the chase is over deep, burning desert sand or bleak, rocky mountain country.

The first examples of the breed were brought to England in the 1830s, when a litter was bred at the London Zoo and a nucleus of breeders began the development of the breed here, but it was not until seven decades later that the Amherstia kennels built up their stock and the Saluki captured the imagination of the show-going public. When it eventually did so, it was to be seen at most hound shows, where it often took top place and attracted great admiration. It was recognised by the Kennel Club in 1922 and by the American Kennel Club in 1927 and, since then, its followers have continued to grow. It is still used in the Middle East in its traditional rôle and, in the West, in hare-coursing where this is allowed, in lure-coursing, and in the cynodromes on the Continent. As with the Afghan and the Sloughi, different types evolved according to the terrain and climate, and these are represented today by two types, the Feathered Saluki and the Smooth Saluki, the latter being found in more southerly parts of Arabia, both types sharing the same points of conformation.

Grace and symmetry are the hallmarks of this well-balanced hound. The expression is one of dignity and faithfulness as it looks at you with gentle, deep, far-seeing eyes. When in action, it is transformed into a legendary spirit of ecstasy, gliding with feathers streaming over the plains like a Pegasus on

Ch Windswift Al Caliph, by Ch Al Caliphs Alyfeh, ex Windswift Khasil, br Miss Watkins, pr Mrs D. Copperthwaite

the wing. Its temperament is superb, friendly and kindly at all times, devoted to its owner's family and safe with children and, like the Sloughi, it is free of odour. It is, of course, a hunter and must be supervised when walked in the country.

The head is beautifully sculptured and held high. It is long and narrow, fairly wide and flat between the ears with a moderate stop, tapering gently to the nose and giving an appearance of great quality. The nose is black or liver. Eyes are dark or hazel, or sometimes, but only rarely, sea-green like those of Minerva, the Goddess of Wisdom. They are well set in, large and oval in shape and with a bright look. The ears are long and furnished with long silky hair in the feathered variety, and they hang close to the skull. The mouth has strong level teeth. The neck is long, supple and muscular.

Forequarters have sloping, well-set-back shoulders, muscular and streamlined. The chest is deep and fairly narrow, with great depth of rib, providing good heart and lung room, and the forelegs are straight and long from the elbow to the knee. The back is fairly broad with muscles slightly arched over the loin. Hindquarters have strong hip bones set wide apart, a good tuck-up, long well-angulated legs, with stifle moderately bent and hocks low to ground, all indicating great galloping and jumping power and maximum litheness.

The feet are strong and supple, of moderate length with long, well-arched toes, not splayed out, yet not cat-footed. The Feathered variety is well feathered between the toes. The tail is set on low and carried naturally in a curve and, although well feathered on the underside, is not bushy. The coat is smooth, soft, shining and of a silky texture. There is slight feathering on the legs, at the back of the thighs, and sometimes a slight woolly feather on thighs and shoulders, except in the Smooth variety. The colours are off-white, cream, fawn, golden, red, grizzle-and-tan, tri-colour (white, black and tan) and black-and-tan, or variations of these colours. Solid black or brindle are not liked.

Height: dogs 23–28 in (58–71 cm); bitches 20–25½ in (51–65 cm).
Weight: relative to height.

Sloughi

At first sight, the Sloughi is often taken for a smooth-coated Saluki, but a closer look reveals that it is heavier, more strongly boned, without feathering and usually distinguishable by typical black markings round the eyes. Closely related to the Saluki and the Afghan Hound, it descends, like them, from the original Greyhound of the plains of the Middle East, making its home with the conquering Arabs in North Africa, mostly in Morocco and the Northern Sahara. Also like the Saluki and Afghan, it was the only dog considered by Arab tribesmen to be worthy of a place in their tents at night; indeed they affectionately called it *el hor*, meaning 'the illustrious one'! It has been pure-bred for centuries and can be seen in practically its present form in ancient carvings of that region and in the hunting-scene mosaics at the Bardo Museum in Tunis. It was apparently a kind of status symbol among the tribes, who vied with each other for the number and quality of the Sloughis they owned, prizing them next only to their beautiful horses. They used it to hunt gazelle, hare and even jackal in the desert where its sandy-coloured coat allowed it to approach close up to the game before its presence was detected. The speed of the chase that followed, and the excitement of the mounted huntsmen, was to be retold afterwards in the tents, choice morsels of the carcasses having been reserved for the hounds at nightfall. It has more recently been used with success for hunting deer in Europe.

There are in fact two types of this hound, the Sloughi of the desert and the Sloughi of the mountains, that of the desert being smaller, slimmer and more finely built, whereas the mountain Sloughi is stronger-boned, closer-coupled and more compact. Otherwise they share the same characteristics and both types can occur in the same litter. This hound is built above all for speed and endurance and the ability to travel great distances in a short time. Like its

Djaeser Djidjiha Etnen from Kamet, by Ch Serdouk, ex Richa Talata, br N. Morland-Austin, pr Miss J. B. Saunders

siblings, it is intelligent, elegant and graceful and fits into the family circle perfectly, without losing any of its original stamina, provided that it is well exercised; it was, in fact, quite capable of looking after itself in the desert for weeks if it managed to get separated from the hunt.

Its expression is one of sadness and nostalgia with a nonchalant indifference towards strangers, but it can be most affectionate towards its master and family, and it makes an excellent guard and watch dog. It is very hardy and enjoys good health and, as an added bonus, it is clean and free of any doggy odour. It has recently received recognition by the Fédération Cynologique Internationale and the Kennel Club as a Moroccan pure-breed.

The general appearance is that of a racy dog with a free and flowing gait and a frame marked by its muscular leanness. The head is fairly strong, but not heavy or with too angular lines; it is, however, heavier than that of the Greyhound. The skull is flat, fairly broad, rounded behind and curving harmoniously into the sides, and the eye sockets protrude only slightly. The frontal bone and the occiput are pronounced; the stop is only slight. The muzzle is wedge-shaped, moderately refined and of the same length as the skull. The nose and lips are black or dark brown. The eyes are large, dark and well set into the orbit, having somewhat oblique and triangular lids. The eye colour in lighter-coloured dogs (off-white, sable, fawn or isabella) is a velvet black with dark eyelashes as if made-up; in dark dogs it is of a burnt topaz shade, i.e. a yellowish amber. Ears are flat and triangular with rounded tips, and not too large. They are folded down close to the head and set level with or slightly above the eye. It is admissible but undesirable to have them carried away from the skull or lightly thrown back. The jaws are strong and the bite scissor. The neck is strong yet elegant, fairly long and well-arched, with slightly loose skin making fine pleats under the throat.

Forequarters have well-laid, clearly visible and moderately oblique shoulders. The forelegs are flat-boned and well muscled. The chest is not too broad and reaches down nearly to the elbow. The tuck-up is good and the topline almost level, with the back fairly short but slightly longer in the bitch. The croup is bony and oblique with prominent haunches. Hindquarters have broad and slightly arched loins, thighs of good length but rather flat and hocks well let down with good angulation.

Feet are thin, of elongated oval shape, with strong black or dark nails. The desert Sloughi is often hare-footed. The tail is thin and well set on, without fringes or long hair. It has a marked curve at the end and reaches the point of the hock. When the dog is moving, the tail must never rise higher than back level.

The coat is short and fine with tough hair. The colours are all shades of sable or fawn, with or without black mask, off-white, brindle, black with tan points, fawn with brindle markings, or a more or less generally dark coat. Solid black or white are admissible but undesirable. Dark coats sometimes have a white patch on the chest. Piebald and skewbald are barred.

Height: Desert type dogs 27½–29½ in (70–75 cm); bitches 25½–27½ in (65–70 cm). Mountain type dogs 23½–25½ in (60–65 cm); bitches 21½–23½ in (55–60 cm).
Weight: relative to height.

Whippet

The origin of the Whippet has been the subject of much controversy over the years. One thing, however, is certain, that is the location, namely the industrial, metallurgical and mining areas of the North-East of England. Although the breed's history stretches over only some 300 years or so, it has become an extremely popular show dog, principally because it is such a good animal to handle in the ring, where it is infallibly on its well-mannered, best behaviour.

The Greyhound in reduced format is clearly the main progenitor, breeding small to small. A touch of Old English White Terrier was no doubt added from time to time to give a bit of fire to an otherwise too gentle a dog. Some naturalists speak of the Pharaoh Hound and the Italian Greyhound as possible outcrosses, but it is unlikely that the working classes who bred it would have gone to the trouble of using imported dogs when excellent material was ready to hand.

It was first shown at Crufts in 1897 and was recognised by the Kennel Club in 1902. Since then its fame has travelled round the world and few shows are without its presence. It has come a long way since the miners of the Newcastle area raced their slender 'rag dogs' on Sunday mornings, with the owners standing waving a rag at one end of a straight track and the dogs racing down towards them after being liberated at the other and finishing up, more often than not, in the arms of their masters. Over a short distance, it is faster even than the Greyhound, being capable of speeds up to 40 mph (65 km/h). Its speed and keenness have been likened to the crack of the whip, hence its name. It is referred to in some documents as the Wappit. Rabbiting was another of the miners' favourite pastimes, providing good sport and a good Sunday dinner at one and the same time.

There were, in the early days, two types of Whippet, the Rough and the Smooth, but the latter became by far the more popular with the growing importance of dog shows, and the rough-coated dog, not recognised by the Kennel Club, is nowadays only seen in the area of its origin at Lurcher meetings. Apart from shows, the smooth-coated Whippet is often seen at stadia, where it races from the trap after an electrically-propelled lure, in the same way as the Greyhound in Europe and America; also in some parts of Britain it is coursed after rabbits.

The Whippet can do 350 m in 23 seconds on the straight. When chasing hare and rabbit, it runs like the wind and can turn on a penny. Its neck should be long and strong to stop it falling when catching its quarry at speed.

The success of the Whippet is largely due to its perfectly sound temperament, completely friendly nature and clean-footedness, making it an ideal dog for the family and fireside, needing only a relatively small amount of food daily, since it has an appetite no bigger than that of a small terrier. It does not want too much exercise either, so long as it gets an occasional workout of short but intense activity. Generally, it is very docile and obedient but, in some specimens, the terrier temperament will show itself from time to time, especially during periods of great excitement.

Beautifully balanced muscular strength, great elegance, graceful symmetrical outline and a powerful gait are the corner-stones of its general appearance. In motion, its action is perfectly free, the forelegs being thrown forward, low over the ground like a thoroughbred horse, not in a hackney-like way. Hindlegs come well under the body giving great propelling power. The general movement must not look stilted, high stepping, short or mincing.

The head is long and lean but proportionally wider than that of the bigger

Ch Cottonmere Monty of Oakbark, by Oakbark Mister Blue, ex Ribblesmere Xmas Carol, br Miss D. M. Greenwood, prs Mr & Mrs D. Meakin

sighthounds; it is flat on top and tapering to the muzzle, fairly wide between the eyes and with powerful, clean-cut jaws. The nose is generally black, but in blue-coloured dogs it can be blue and in livers it may be liver; white or parti-coloured dogs can have a butterfly nose. Eyes are bright with a very alert expression. Ears are rose-shaped, small and of fine texture. The teeth are strong, with top teeth fitting closely over the bottom. The neck is long, muscular and elegantly arched.

Forequarters have oblique muscular shoulders with the blades carried up to the spine and closely set together at the top. Forelegs are straight and upright with not too wide a front. Pasterns are strong with a slight spring; elbows are well set under the body. The chest is very deep with plenty of heart and lung room. The brisket is deep and well defined. The ribs are well sprung. The back is broad, well muscled, firm and rather long with a definite arch over the loin but not humped, giving an impression of strength and power. Hindquarters are strong and broad across the thighs. Stifles and hocks are well bent and second thighs strong, enabling the dog to stand over a lot of ground and showing great driving power.

Feet are very neat, well split up between the toes, with highly arched knuckles and thick strong pads. The tail is long and tapering and without feathering; when the dog is in movement, it is carried in a delicate curve upwards but not over the back. The coat is short, as close as possible and fine in texture. Any colour or combination of colours is allowed, the golden tiger-brindles and silver fawns being especially eye-catching.

Height: dogs 18½ in (47 cm) ideally; bitches 17½ in (44 cm) ideally.
Slight variation in height is admissible. The American standard specifies a dog of slightly greater stature: dogs 19–22 in (48–56 cm) and bitches 18–21 in (46–53 cm).
Weight: relative to height.

Lurcher

The Lurcher is a carefully worked-out cross-breed. The growing popularity of this dog is really astonishing; it has been estimated that there are now more than 5,000 Lurchers in Great Britain! It is first and foremost a sporting and working dog, which can catch fox and deer as well as rabbit and hare, but it is also a marvellous companion, affectionate, calm, beautiful and full of dignity. More precisely, it is a studied cross, combining speed and intelligence: the speed of the sighthound and the intelligence of the sheepdog.

It has become more and more popular in Britain, especially among the hunting and racing fraternities, although, of course, it is not recognised by the Kennel Club. It is to be seen at the country fêtes and sports organised in the summer months by hunt supporters' clubs, where classes are put on for Jack Russells, as well as Lurchers. The first Lurcher show took place at Lambourne in Berkshire in 1971 and now some fifty shows a year are held. When the judging is over, the principal events of the day begin, namely the racing fixtures. Whilst the Jack Russells run after a fox's brush pulled in front of them at the end of a cord, the Lurchers chase a stuffed rabbit worked by an electric motor, just as Greyhounds do at the stadium.

The excitement of the spectators, who come from all parts of the county and neighbouring counties, is really a sight worth seeing. Among the Range Rovers, Land-Rovers and shooting-breaks are little cars and old trucks of all kinds; the sport of Lurcher-racing counts among its adherents members of all classes of society: the squire of the village with his lady and the Master of Foxhounds, as well as the gardener, the game-keeper, the gypsy . . . and the poacher!

It is, indeed, largely to the poacher that we owe the creation of the Lurcher of today: the word *lur* in the Romany tongue means 'thief'. Since the seventeenth century, we find in English literature references to the poacher with his Lurcher which he used for catching rabbits and hares. Another equally exciting sport is Lurcher-coursing, in which pairs of dogs are set in pursuit of a hare in an enclosed field.

66

Gertrude Madach, br/pr Mr J. Chisnall

Lurchers are classified in two groups, according to height at the withers: under or over 22 in (56 cm). In order to produce the best results, the general practice is to mate a male sighthound with a female sheepdog. For the big Lurcher, the formula is Greyhound × Rough Collie; and, for the small variety, Whippet × Border Collie. Very often, especially in Scotland, the Greyhound is replaced by the Deerhound, and the Border Collie by the Shetland Sheepdog. One can equally well use a female sighthound and a male sheepdog. It is important, for aesthetic reasons, to choose a male and a female of similar coloration. For the small variety, the formulae black-and-white Whippet × black-and-white Border Collie, and red-and-white Whippet × tri-colour-Shetland Sheepdog, produce puppies of striking beauty which resemble young Borzois.

Some enthusiasts prefer to accentuate the sighthound type and use the formula: ¾ sighthound + ¼ sheepdog, i.e. sighthound × sighthound/ sheepdog in the second generation. For example, in the Eastern counties, where dogs have to work a difficult terrain, one finds above all the type of cross ¾ Greyhound + ¼ Deerhound, i.e. all sighthound, which produces a type which never tires. But for easier, shorter terrain, a small Lurcher, ¾ Whippet + ¼ Border Collie, is more suitable as it can turn and change direction more easily than the bigger dog without losing too much speed.

In Scotland, the formula ¾ Greyhound or Whippet + ¼ Golden Retriever (or a straight cross, Greyhound × Golden Retriever) is popular for catch and retrieve, producing a beautiful, well-balanced animal and in the Midlands, they enthuse over another cross: ¾ Whippet + ¼ Bedlington. But, as Phil Drabble, the well-known writer, journalist and television personality told me recently, it is always a question of 'horses for courses', that is to say that one chooses the formula which suits best the terrain of the region where the dog is intended to work.

Height: large type over 22 in (56 cm); small type under 22 in (56 cm).
Weight: relative to height.

Terriers

Airedale Terrier

The King of Terriers — a well-earned title for the biggest dog in the group, the Airedale. Originating in the valley of the River Aire in Yorkshire, it was used with packs of hounds to hunt the otter, which, in the mid-nineteenth century, was to be found in great numbers on the banks of the Aire and the Wharfe. As the hounds were reluctant to follow the otter to its watery burrow, the local terrier men, who needed a big terrier which could keep up with the hounds, decided to cross their broken-coated black-and-tan terriers with otterhounds. The occasional addition of other blood, such as Welsh, Irish, Kerry Blue and the old-type Bedlington, tipped the balance in favour of the terrier type and resulted in a strong, game, tireless dog ideal for the task, without equal for hunting the otter, and bigger quarry, such as the badger and even the wild boar in those well-forested countries where this formidable adversary still exists. It will even work as a gun dog and retrieve wild fowl when required. (Badger-digging was banned in 1981 by an amendment to the 1973 Badger Protection Act.)

The Waterside or Bingley Terrier, as it was first called, bred true to type and soon became known as the Airedale, after the Great Airedale Show where it created such a favourable impression in 1879. It was recognised by the Kennel Club in 1886 and a breed club was formed not long afterwards. Its courage, intelligence and versatility attracted a wider circle of admirers and its qualities as a formidable guard and defence dog led to its adoption by the railways, customs, port authorities, police and the armed forces. In World War 1, Airedales were used by both Allied and German armies as patrol, tracker and messenger dogs, and helped the Red Cross in the task of finding the wounded. Between the wars, Lieutenant Colonel Richardson was a noted breeder of Airedale guard dogs trained to face up to small-arms fire. During World War 2, an Airedale bitch called Alma guided men of the Civil Defence to the rescue of numerous people trapped in a cellar after a V2 bombardment and was decorated by the authorities for this act of valour . . . a truly noble dog! As a handsome companion and fearless protector, it is unique and its extrovert style makes it outstanding in the show rings of today.

Of symmetrical proportions, the Airedale has a long, well-balanced head with a flat skull, narrowing slightly towards small dark eyes and with hardly any stop. The jaws are powerful and the bite level, closing like a vice, strength of foreface being an essential point. Lips are tight and the nose is black. Ears

Ch Jokyl Gallipants, by Ch Siccawei Galliard, ex Ch Jokyl Smartie Pants, br Wundpets, prs Mrs O. Jackson & Mrs M. Swash

are V-shaped, smallish and carried to the side, with the topline of the fold above skull level and not hanging houndlike. The neck is muscular, of moderate length and without dewlap.

Forequarters have long well-laid-back shoulders, with flat blades sloping into the back. The well-boned forelegs are straight and parallel to each other with elbows perpendicular to the body and working freely. The body is strong and short-coupled and the chest deep without being broad.

Hindquarters are long with muscular thighs and good bend of stifle. The hocks are well let down and parallel when viewed from the rear. The feet are small, round and compact with good, deep, well-cushioned pads and are the same distance apart as the elbows and hocks. The toes are moderately arched. The tail is set high, carried gaily, strong and not docked too short.

The coat is dense, wiry and close-lying. The soft, short undercoat is covered by a hard outercoat which can be straight or slightly wavy, careful stripping by hand being necessary for show presentation. Its colour is black or dark grizzle on the body and light tan elsewhere, with darker shades on the ears and sides of the skull. The more intense colorations these days are usually to be found in the Midlands, particularly in Staffordshire.

Height: dogs 23–24 in (58–61 cm); bitches 22–23 in (56–58 cm).
Weight: dogs 55 lb (24.9 kg); bitches 48 lb (21.8 kg).

Australian Terrier

The Australian Terrier originated around Melbourne and is the result of crosses between the local broken-coated terriers and various short-legged dogs that had been brought in to Victoria, Tasmania and New South Wales by the original settlers from Scotland. There is strong evidence that the Scottish terriers all contributed to its make-up; its coat indicates Skye ancestors and it clearly gets its silky topknot from the Dandie Dinmont. Some old-type Yorkshire Terrier blood, and perhaps even a touch of Manchester Terrier, was added to intensify coloration, and no doubt the Silky Terrier from Sydney also contributed to its development.

Known as the Blue-and-Tan Terrier when it was shown in the early 1870s, it gained in status when the Australian Terrier breed club was formed in Melbourne in 1889. A red- or sandy-coated strain was evolved in Adelaide by the MacFarlanes, who introduced a reddish Cairn outcross. Australian Terriers were brought to England in 1896 and were shown intermittently in the early twentieth century, being recognised by the Kennel Club in 1933.

Although one of the smallest in the terrier group — an honour shared with the Norfolk and Norwich Terriers — the Australian Terrier has the true terrier characteristics and is a keen hunter of vermin; it was used as a watch dog in the lonely homesteads of the outback. The tough settlers appreciated its ability as a rabbiter and rat-killer. The modern dog, however, is a more sophisticated companion, neat, hardy, intelligent and of even temperament; it is always eager to please, full of the joy of living and very suited to town life as it is not given to unnecessary barking. It is a real terrier and, like the Scottie, full of its own importance and sure to attract the attention of all who come in contact with it. Another point in its favour is that its coat is easily kept in good order, needing only the minimum of grooming for show purposes.

A short-legged terrier, it gives an appearance of tough sturdiness with the real terrier look. The head is long and has a moderately wide, flat skull with a slight but noticeable stop. The muzzle is strong and of the same length as the skull, and the nose is black. The small, dark brown eyes are set fairly well apart. The ears are erect, small and pointed and free from long hair. The jaws are powerful with a scissor bite and tight black lips. The long, slightly-arched neck is shapely, strong and adorned with a frill.

Forequarters have long, well-laid shoulders and the forelegs are straight and parallel. Pasterns are strong, without slope and only slightly feathered to the knee. The body is long in proportion to the height, the ribs are well sprung, and the chest is of moderate depth. The topline is level, the loins are strong and the flanks deep. Hindquarters are of moderate length, broad, with

Ch Jeken Blondin, by Jeken Troubadour, ex Sunnyland Kennel Sheila, br/pr Miss N. K. Elwin

muscular thighs, stifles well turned and hocks well bent, let down and parallel.

The feet are small, well padded, closely knit and moderately arched, turning neither in nor out, and with strong black or dark toe-nails. The tail is docked not too short, set high and carried gaily, but not over the back.

The coat is harsh, straight and dense, about 2½ in (6.35 cm) long with a short, soft undercoat. The muzzle, lower legs and feet have short hair. The colour is light or dark blue with rich tan on the face and ears, under the body, on the lower legs and feet and around the vent. Clear sandy or red is an alternative colour. The topknot is lighter than the head in each case.

Height: dogs 10 in (25 cm); bitches 9 in (23 cm).
Weight: dogs 14 lb (6.4 kg); bitches 12 lb (5.4 kg).

Bedlington Terrier

A terrier from the lands near the Scottish Border and bred in the first instance by wandering gypsies along with their Lurchers and longdogs, the

Ch Brickbats Broughton, by Wilnesden Silver, ex Blue Print of Tiddly Mount, br Mr S. M. Edwards, pr Mr C. A. Smallwood

Bedlington Terrier is closely related to the Dandie Dinmont and shares with it two distinctive characteristics which no other terriers have — long ears and topknots. Known as the 'poor man's dog', the Bedlington was later adopted by the collier fraternity of Northumberland, who used it principally for rabbiting and for ratting down the mines. A touch of Bull Terrier from Staffordshire, some local Border Terrier and even Otterhound blood resulted in a formidable, sporting, multi-purpose terrier, equally good for catching a rabbit for the Sunday dinner as for winning a bet in the dog-fighting pit. It gets its name from the village of Bedlington near Rothbury in Northumberland where Joe Ainsley, a mason by trade, began to fix the type of these dogs in the first quarter of the nineteenth century. He crossed a local Rothbury ratter called Old Piper with his bitch Phoebe in 1825 to produce the forerunners of the dog we know today, some Whippet blood being introduced at a later stage to give the much appreciated speed and racy lines, and a touch of Dandie Dinmont for added gameness and strength; the progeny were called Bedlington Terriers.

Great interest was shown in the breed at dog shows in the early 1870s and this led to the formation of the National Bedlington Terrier Club in 1877, with the object of promoting its development and popularity. Indeed the evolution of this northern breed is such that the dog we see in the ring today bears but little resemblance to the original. Although perhaps a little standoffish in temperament and distrustful of other dogs, it is easy to train and makes a good house dog, barking only when necessary to sound the alert. Seeming at first sight rather delicate, it is in fact very strong and dead game.

The appearance of the Bedlington is not unlike that of the sprinter — lithe, lean and graceful with the hidden power of a coiled spring. The head is pear-shaped, with a narrow rounded skull, and the jaw is long and tapering. The line from the occiput to the nose is straight and without stop. The foreface is well filled up below the eyes. The lips are tight without flews and the nostrils are large. Blues and blue-and-tans have black noses, livers and sandies have brown noses. The eyes are small, sunken and of triangular appearance. Blues have dark eyes, blue-and-tans have eyes of a lighter shade with amber lights, while livers and sandies have light hazel eyes. Ears are moderate in size, almond-shaped, set on low and hanging flat to the cheek. They are covered with short fine hair with a fringe of whitish silky hair at the tip. The teeth are strong and level. The neck is long and tapering, carrying the head high.

Forequarters are straight but wider apart at the chest than at the feet. Shoulders are flat and pasterns are long and slightly sloping. The body is muscular, flexible and well ribbed up, and the chest is deep and broad. The back is roached and the loin arched and muscular.

Hindquarters are of moderate length and, because of the roached back and arched loin, the hindlegs look longer than the forelegs. The hocks are strong and well let down.

The Bedlington has long hare feet, compact and well padded. The tail is undocked and of moderate length, thick at the root, tapering to a point and curving gracefully. It is set on low.

The coat, which requires skilful trimming, is really striking and distinctive, having a sculptured effect when the dog is presented in the ring. It is thick and linty in texture, non-shedding and standing out from the skin, and with a tendency to twist on the head and face. The colours are blue, blue-and-tan, liver or sandy, and all Bedlingtons have a profuse, silky, nearly-white topknot.

Height: dogs 16½ in (42 cm); bitches 15½ in (39 cm).
Weight: dogs 20–23 lb (9.1–10.4 kg); bitches 18–21 lb (8.2–9.5 kg).

Border Terrier

Like the Bedlington Terrier, the Border Terrier comes from Northumberland. The huntsmen of the Border Hunt produced the breed in the mid-nineteenth century from old-type Bedlington, Lakeland and Dandie

Ch Farmway Snow Kestrel, by Farmway Woodpecker, ex Farmway Snow Finch, br/pr Mrs M. Aspinwall

Dinmont crosses to suit the particular needs of the kind of country in which they hunted. They needed a small robust dog, well able to accompany the pack in the difficult rocky terrain and game enough to bolt the large grey hill fox that went to ground or holed up among the boulders and rocks of the Cheviot hills. Interest in the breed was renewed at the turn of the century and the terrier grew in popularity after World War 1. A standard was drawn up by descendants of the original breeders in 1920; a breed club was formed and recognition was secured from the Kennel Club in 1921. The Border Terrier is now seen in good numbers at championship shows and its many qualities are increasing its popularity in the United States of America and in Australia.

The conformation of the little terrier enables it to fulfil all the requirements of the hunts of the Border region — a leg long enough to permit it to keep up with the hounds but short enough to allow it to go to ground, a slender rib cage to facilitate manoeuvrability at close quarters, a weatherproof coat and, above all, a steady but fearless temperament and the toughness to ensure survival if cut off in this bleak part of the country.

It is the most workmanlike and natural of show terriers in present times, a first-class hunt terrier, and also, loving plenty of exercise, it makes a very fine and long-lived companion for an active person. It is an excellent watch dog for farm or country residence, yet it is not out of place in the town, as long as it gets a good daily workout in a park or open space. But of course it is happiest when running with the hounds or walking in the hills for hours on end with the huntsman. It is an excellent family dog, being especially good with children, and equally important is its friendliness towards other dogs and especially the hounds it loves to work with.

The head of the Border Terrier is best described as being otter-like, moderately broad in the skull and with a short but strong muzzle. A black nose is preferred, but a liver- or flesh-coloured one is admitted. The eyes are dark with a keen expression, and full of courage.

The small ears are V-shaped, moderately thick and dropping forward close to the cheek. The bite is preferably scissor, with the upper incisors slightly overlapping the lower, but a level mouth is quite acceptable. Undershot or overshot mouths constitute major faults in this working terrier. The neck is strong and of moderate length.

Forequarters have straight, medium-boned forelegs and the body is deep, narrow and fairly long, with ribs carried well back but not oversprung; the terrier can be spanned with both hands behind the shoulder. Hindquarters are racy and have strong loins and thighs with straight hindlegs.

The feet are small and thickly padded. The tail is undocked, moderately short and fairly thick at the base; it is set high and carried gaily, but not curled over the back, tapering to a point.

The coat is harsh and dense with a close-knit undercoat over a thickish skin. The colours are red, wheaten, grizzle-and-tan, or blue-and-tan. The wheaten shade is not seen quite so often these days, but any prejudice formerly shown against the blue has now finally disappeared.

Height: dogs 13 in (33 cm); bitches 12 in (30 cm).
Weight: dogs 13 – 15½ lb (5.9 – 7 kg); bitches 11½ – 14 lb (5.2 – 6.4 kg).

Bull Terriers

The Bull Terrier (Standard). The Bill Sykes dog, the matador of the ring, the gladiator — all titles earned by the Bull Terrier. Having said that, we must at once add that there is no dog more gentle with children.

Bull-baiting was one of the so-called sports indulged in by certain sections of the British public in the eighteenth and first part of the nineteenth centuries. Finally, people had become so sickened by the spectacle of mangled dogs that baiting was outlawed in 1835. It was replaced by straight dog-fights. These were reminiscent of cock-fights, the two dogs being thrown into a pit and wagers laid on the likely winner. The Bulldogs were found to be too clumsy and heavy to manoeuvre in the pits and so they were crossed

Ch Abraxus Audacity, the only Bull Terrier to date to become Supreme Champion at Crufts, br/pr Mrs V. Drummond-Dick

with terriers. Eventually these fights were also banned and the fighting had to be done clandestinely. The fights took place mostly in the London region, in the Midlands and in the West Country. It was in 1860 that James Hinks of Birmingham first showed his strain of White Bull Terriers, the result of crosses between the Bulldog and the Old English White Terrier; they soon earned the name of 'white cavaliers'. Another breeder called Preston introduced Whippet, Dalmatian and Pointer blood. A further possible cross was with the Collie and it could be that it gets its dolichocephale (arching) forehead from this source. When Hinks was accused of having sacrificed the dog's fighting spirit for a better appearance, he challenged all comers to fight his bitch Puss for a wager of £5 and a case of champagne. A match was arranged at Long Acre in London, and, after half-an-hour, Puss had killed her opponent without much damage to herself . . . indeed next day she won first prize in the show ring!

The 'new' Bull Terrier soon became more popular as a show dog than its fighting cousins. In the 1920s, colour, especially brindle, was brought back into the Hinks' strain in order to combat the tendency to deafness which the all-white dogs had developed. It was at the height of its popularity in the post-World War 2 years and was used as a police dog and also as a hunting dog in

Africa. It is said to prefer a male owner and, of course, its great strength makes it a more suitable companion for a man. Its ability to stand the heat endeared it to the British Civil Service in tropical climates. Indeed Old Bodger, the Bull Terrier featured in *The Incredible Journey* by Sheila Burnford epitomises all that is good in the character of this fine terrier.

The general appearance of the Bull Terrier is that of an exceptionally strong, muscular dog of symmetrical proportions and determined, courageous and intelligent expression, together with an even temperament. In motion, this dog covers the ground with free easy strides and a jaunty air, the forelegs and hindlegs moving parallel to each other, the forelegs reaching out well and the hindlegs flexing at the stifle and hock with great thrust.

The head is long and strong, egg-shaped and free from indentations. The skull is almost flat from ear to ear; the profile curves gently down from the top of the skull to the tip of the nose, which is black and bent down at the tip. The eyes appear narrow, oblique and triangular, well sunken, very dark and piercing. The distance from tip of nose to eyes is greater than from the eyes to the top of the skull. The ears are small, thin and close together, the dog being able to hold them erect. The mouth is strong and teeth regular with scissor bite; lips are tight. The neck is long, arched and muscular, tapering from shoulders to head, with no loose skin.

Forequarters are muscular, the shoulder blades wide, close to the chest and sloping backwards. The forelegs have strong round bone and are moderately long and parallel. Elbows are held straight and pasterns are upright. The ribs are well sprung with great depth from withers to brisket. The back is short with level topline behind the withers but roaching slightly over the loin. The underline curves upwards from brisket to belly. The chest is broad.

Hindquarters have strong muscular legs, with well-bent stifle and well-angulated hock, not quite so well boned as the front; they are parallel when viewed from behind.

The feet are round and compact and the toes are well arched. The tail is undocked, short, set on low, carried horizontally and tapering to a fine point.

The coat is short, flat and even with a fine gloss, fitting tightly. The colour is pure white, or white with head markings, or coloured with a little white, brindle being preferred.

Mr Raymond H. Oppenheimer's dog, Bar Sinister, was considered the greatest of all Bull Terriers, and, although unable to be shown because of his being partly cryptorchid, he was an outstanding sire.

Height and weight: there are no height or weight limits, but there should be an impression of maximum substance in relation to height.

The Bull Terrier (Miniature). The Miniature Bull Terrier is a facsimile of its big brother in all respects, with the single exception of size. It was first recognised as a separate variety by the Kennel Club in 1943 and the breed standard was published in the same year. Fortunately, it has never suffered from the drawbacks of miniaturisation. Indeed disparities of weight in the old-type bulldogs were sometimes as much as 40 lb (18 kg). In some litters, puppies were found to be three times the size of others. The present-day Miniature Bull Terrier has been produced by selective mating of small examples of the breed. The general impression should be one of maximum substance in relation to the size of the dog, giving a well-balanced effect.

Height: dogs 14 in (36 cm); bitches 12 in (30 cm).
Weight: dogs 20 lb (9.1 kg); bitches 18 lb (8.2 kg).

Cairn Terrier

A brave little terrier from the Western Isles and Highlands of Scotland, the lairds' favourite in Argyllshire and the Hebrides, the Cairn Terrier is to be seen everywhere in those parts. With its long-haired cousin, the Skye Terrier, it forms the rootstock of all the Scottish terriers. The word Cairn signifies, in Scotland, a heap of stones covering the tumuli or sepulchral mounds left by

Sandaig Souvenir, by Ch Ugadale Leadall, ex Sandaig Sorrel, br/pr Mrs P. Jeffrey

the Roman invaders on the moorlands after their defeat by the Scots. Foxes and rabbits took refuge in the brush which eventually covered the cairns and the little terriers which hunted them found their name in this way. In 1600, James VI of Scotland sent a few couples as a present to the Court of France, and the Highland chieftains all had their little packs of terriers, the ancestors of the modern dogs, to use against fox, badger and otter.

From the seventeenth century, the MacDonalds bred their own strains of Cairn Terrier, as did the MacLeods of Drynoch on the Isle of Skye, and, in fact, when the first Cairns were shown at Inverness, they were known as Short-Haired Skye Terriers. It was Martin MacLeod who took his pack of Cairns with him when he emigrated to Canada in 1840 and their popularity in the New World soon became established. In the Inverness Art Gallery, there is a picture by Rosa Bonheur, dated 1845, showing a typical Cairn. Indeed the mascot of the Aberdeen cricket team towards the end of the nineteenth century was a little Cairn. It was not until 1912, however, that the Kennel Club first classified as a Cairn Terrier a dog called Nisbet, belonging to a Major Ewing. In 1922, there were 141 dogs of the breed registered at the Kennel Club.

It is the least changed in appearance over the years of all the terriers of Scotland; it is a most intelligent and companionable little fellow. It is not surprising therefore that the Duke of Windsor, a great dog-lover, should have chosen it as his favourite breed alongside the Pug.

Of a fearless and sportive disposition, the Cairn is game, hardy and easily trained. It has a shaggy look, yet is not difficult to keep tidy; it is strong and compact and very free in movement.

The head is small, but in proportion to the body, and gives a generally foxy appearance. The skull is broad, the stop well defined and the muzzle powerful but not heavy. The eyes are set wide apart with a definite indentation between them; they are rather sunken and dark hazel in colour. The eyebrows are shaggy. The ears are small and pointed, not too closely set. They are carried well and erect. The jaws are strong and the teeth large with level bite; the nose and lips are very dark. The neck is well set on and of medium length.

Forequarters have sloping shoulders and a moderate length of leg with fairly good bone. The forelegs and elbows are straight and parallel. The body is compact and the back is straight, of medium length and well coupled. The ribs are deep and well sprung and hindquarters are very strong.

The forefeet are larger than the hindfeet and may be slightly turned out, with thick strong pads, and the dog stands well forward on his forepaws. The short tail is undocked, carried gaily and erect when in action.

The coat is of great importance. The weatherproof outercoat is profuse and hard whilst the furry undercoat is short, soft and close. The hair on the head and forehead is full, as on the tail and legs, but not on the ears. The colours are red, sandy, grey, brindle or almost black. Dark points on ears and muzzle are typical.

In the newly revised standard, the ideal weight for a Cairn is given as 14–16 lb (6.35–7.25 kg) and the gait is described as a free-flowing stride, with forelegs reaching well forward and hindlegs giving strong propulsion.

Height: dogs 10 in (25 cm); bitches 9 in (23 cm).
Weight: dogs 14 lb (6.4 kg); bitches 13 lb (5.9 kg).

Dandie Dinmont Terrier

Also from the country adjoining the Scottish Border with England comes the Dandie Dinmont Terrier. Gainsborough included a Dandie Dinmont in his portrait of the third Duke of Buccleuch, painted in 1770, but the breed dates back to the early eighteenth century and originated, like the Bedlington, with the Romany nomads, who were frequently to be seen in those parts. Many are the stories about these gypsy families, especially the Allens, Andersons and Cammells and their meetings two or three times a year to match their dogs against each other in pursuit of fox, badger or wild cat in the Cheviots. Others interested in the dog sport took up the breed, which had now begun to be known as the Piper Allen Terrier, after Gypsy Piper Allen who was noted for his many hair-raising exploits at that time.

The Davidson family of Hawick also began to breed seriously and developed the pepper-and-mustard strain, and it was Sir Walter Scott who immortalised the 'game wee dogs', and their breeder Jim Davidson, a farmer of Lyndlea, on whom he modelled the character Yeoman Dandie Dinmont in his novel *Guy Mannering*, first published in 1814. Indeed this is the only breed of dog named after a character in literature. As so often happens with publicity of this kind, the popularity of the breed took off from then on and everybody wanted a Dandie Dinmont. Like the Bedlington and the Border Terrier, the Dandie Dinmont took its place in the show ring and the conformation of the dog has changed little since the breed standard was first formulated in 1876. Scott, who kept a couple of these terriers himself, described them as 'very desirable companions'. The Davidson pack of terriers was well known to him and always had the words 'pepper or mustard' in their names, as did Scott's own in his novel. He said of them that they 'fear nothing that ever cam' wi' a hairy skin on't'. Selective breeding has produced a terrier quite dissimilar to other terriers, with flowing, curving lines and arching back.

The appearance of the Dandie at first sight could be described as rather quaint or even funny. But this would bely its character, which is that of a bold

Ch Hendell Tiaella of Blaven, by Blaven Baretta, ex Hendell Minetta, br Mrs P. D. Hulme, prs Mr & Mrs D. M. Murray

tireless extrovert with a loud bark that makes it a good house dog. Its head in fact seems too big for its body; this is due to the broad skull and domed forehead, crowned with a topknot of soft silky hair which also covers the face and muzzle. The nose is black and there is a distinctive, bare, triangular patch between the nose and the eyes. The dark hazel eyes are large, round and full of character. The ears, pendulous and set low and well back, tapering almost to a point, harmonise with the body colour but are a shade darker and have a feathering of lighter hair. The bite is level, the teeth exceptionally strong and large. The neck is muscular and well set into the shoulders.

Forequarters have short legs, well boned and set wide apart, the chest being well let down between. The legs are feathered behind in a lighter colour than in front. The body is long and flexible and the ribs well sprung and round. The back is rather low at the shoulders, having a slight downward curve leading to a corresponding arch over the loins dropping to the root of the tail.

Hindquarters have muscular legs, somewhat longer than the forelegs and set wider apart giving a look of solidity. The thighs are well developed and without feathering.

The forefeet are much larger than the hindfeet and are tan-coloured in the case of the pepper dog and, in the case of the mustard, they are of a darker shade than the head. The shortish tail is curved like a scimitar and carried gaily, being of medium setting.

The coat has hair about 2 in (5 cm) long from the skull to the tail in a hard and soft mixture. On the underparts, it is softer and lighter in colour. The colours are pepper, ranging from a bluish black to a silver grey, the medium shades being preferred, or mustard ranging from reddish brown to pale fawn with a creamy-shaded head. A touch of white on the chest is quite usual.

Height: dogs 10−11 in (25−28 cm); bitches 8−10 in (20−25 cm).
Weight: dogs 17−18 lb (7.7−8.1 kg); bitches 16−17 lb (7.3−7.7 kg).

Fox Terriers (Smooth and Wire)

In the early days of fox-hunting, the terriers that were used were mostly the brown or black-and-tan types bred especially to work with the pack. It was soon found, however, that their colours were too similar to that of the fox and terriers were getting killed by mistake. By crossing these working terriers with the Beagle, the Old English White Terrier and the Bulldog, dogs with dominant white coats were produced. The Bulldog traits were eventually bred out to eliminate certain recurring faults. Classes for the white Fox Terriers were included at the Birmingham Show in 1862, and from then on the popularity of the breed soared. All the ancestors of the breed came from the best known fox-hunting kennels of the second half of the nineteenth century — Joe from the Belvoir Hunt, Old Jock from the Grove Hunt and

(Smooth) Ch Eclipse of Roxway, by Roxway Encore, ex Roxway Enterprise, br Mr R. W. Davey, prs Mr & Mrs Christisson

(Wire) Ch Blackdale Anticipation, by Int Ch Blackdale Aristocrat, ex Edens Empress, br/pr Mr H. O'Donoghue

Old Trap from the Oakley Hunt. The bitch Nettle, from the Grove Hunt, has also left her mark on the breed. A standard was drawn up in 1876 by the Fox Terrier breed club and has hardly changed over the years, except in respect of size, which is now 18 lb (8.2 kg) maximum instead of 20 lb (9 kg). The Smooths were separately registered and, until the end of World War 1, Smooth Fox Terriers were the top terriers in the popularity stakes, upstanding in the rings like fine porcelain figurines, high favourites of gentlemen of the fancy. The early Fox Terriers had included broken-coated dogs, but it was not until the turn of the century that the Wire-Haired Terrier as we now know it appeared, when the Duchess of Newcastle brought out her Champion Crackler of Notts, who himself sired many champions and was the most influential progenitor of the Wire variety. It was in 1920 that the Wires took over from the Smooths as the most popular breed in Britain, this being largely due to the acceptance of trimming, and meticulously trimmed Wires are still among the show stars of today.

The Smooth and Wire Fox Terriers share an identical conformation. The general appearance is one of perfect symmetry, in fact the symmetry of the Foxhound, standing, as the Kennel Club states, like a 'cleverly made hunter' and clearly able to cover a lot of ground during a day's hunting.

The head is well balanced with the skull and foreface of practically equal length. The skull is flat and narrowing towards the eyes and the stop is slight. The jaw is strong and muscular, the muzzle tapering to a black nose. The eyes are dark, small, round and set fairly deep; they should glint with fire when the dog is roused. The small ears are V-shaped and droop forward close to the cheek. The jaws are strong and the bite level. The neck is fairly long, muscular and gradually widening to the shoulders.

Forequarters have long, well-laid-back shoulders, sloping down from the neck towards fine points with clear-cut withers. The chest is deep and not too broad. The legs are straight and strongly boned, the elbows hanging perpendicular to the sides. The back is short and level and the loins muscular and arched, the back ribs deep, and the whole well ribbed up.

Hindquarters are strong and muscular, free from droop or crouch, with long powerful thighs. The stifles are well curved and the hock joints well bent and parallel viewed from the rear, allowing the dog to move with a straight-through action.

Feet are round, compact and well padded and the toes are moderately arched. The tail is set on high and carried gaily with a three-quarters dock.

The coat of the smooth variety is straight, flat, hard and dense. There should be no bareness on belly or under thighs. The Wire's coat resembles coconut matting, dense, twisting and wiry, with a short soft undercoat; the hair is hardest on back and quarters. As far as colour is concerned, white should predominate. Brindle, red, liver or slaty blue are objectionable. Smooths are usually white with black or tan markings and Wires are often hound-marked or tri-colour.

Height: dogs 15½ in (39 cm); bitches 14½ in (37 cm).
Weight: dogs 16–18 lb (7.3–8.2 kg); bitches 15–17 lb (6.8–7.7 kg).

Glen of Imaal Terrier

The Glen of Imaal Terrier, out in the wilderness for so long, its origins being swathed in the grey mists of the legends of Erin, and its history handed down mostly by word of mouth, was not recognised by the Irish Kennel Club until 1933 when it was first exhibited in Dublin on St Patrick's day, although it was in fact noted in George Turberville's *Noble art de la vénerie ou chasse à courre* as early as 1575. It is now recognised by the English Kennel Club and the Fédération Cynologique Internationale, and has at last found its way to Crufts, where it is, however, the only terrier classified as a rare breed.

It is a native of the mountainous region of County Wicklow and comes from the Glen of Imaal which lies to the South-East of Knockanarrigan. First and foremost a real working terrier of very powerful build, being employed

Malsville Suspicious Mind of Ceysta, by Eversley Patrick, ex Sammac Pippa Girl at Laureat, brs Mr & Mrs Gay, prs Lady Malpas & Rev. Stacey

against fox, otter and badger, it was very often used like the Bull Terriers for dog-fighting at matches held in the backyards of inns or in remote open fields. As intrepid as the Stafford, it totally ignores any injuries it might receive in action. It is now getting better known outside its country of origin and its qualities of great toughness, indomitable courage and dead gameness in a tight corner are becoming more widely appreciated in hunting circles. The working characteristics of the Glen are of paramount importance and, in Eire, in order to be eligible for the title of Champion, a dog has needed to obtain the Teastas Meisneac certificate of proof that it is game to fox and badger.

One of the oldest of native Irish breeds, it is closely related to the Soft-Coated Wheaten and the Kerry Blue, having a coat of similar texture to both which takes some time to reach its fullness. Puppies reach full height of between 12½ and 14 in (31.75 and 35.5 cm) at 6 to 9 months of age, when their development into mature adults begins. The Irish Kennel Club standard permits some coat trimming which amounts only to a general tidying up of the hair on the ears, around the eyes, on the tail and feet in order to produce a good outline.

Glens are able to mix well with other terriers, but they do have the fiery temperament of Irish terriers and never refuse a fight when one is offered but do not necessarily start one. Although extroverts, they are not noisy but have a deterrent deep-throated voice when roused, and make excellent children's guards and gentle companions, loving to follow them into the water. They are now proving themselves good performers in obedience classes. A breed club was formed in 1981 and the Glen made its debut on the British show scene at the London and Home Counties Terrier Club show in November of that year, where the breed had its own classes recognised by the Kennel Club.

Its general appearance is that of a dog of great strength for its size, very active and agile and low-to-ground, with a coat of moderate length and lovely colour and texture. Its movement is free as it covers the ground effortlessly and purposefully.

The head is of good width and fairly long with a pronounced stop; the powerful foreface tapers to the nose. The eyes are dark brown and placed well apart, with a keen expression. The ears are rose or half-pricked and of medium size. The teeth are strong and large and the jaws punishing, with the upper incisors slightly overlapping the lower in a scissor bite. A level mouth is not, however, considered a fault.

The neck is muscular and of moderate length, and the shoulders are well laid back. Forequarters are very powerful with a wide chest and very heavily boned short legs which are slightly bowed and splayed. The straight topline rises slightly to the rump.

Hindquarters are strong, the body deep and longer than it is high, with well-sprung ribs and muscular hips, loins and thighs. Hocks are straight viewed from the rear and hindlegs have great powers of propulsion. Feet are compact, round and well padded. The tail is strong at the insertion, well set on and carried gaily; it is docked with enough left to grasp when fully grown.

The coat is not more than 4 in (10 cm) long, wiry in texture in the topcoat with a soft undercoat. Its colour is all the shades of wheaten (from light wheaten to golden red), blue, blue-grey and blue-brindle, but not toning to black. The coloration has been likened to a kind of mountain camouflage, blue like the heather and golden wheaten like the gorse. Puppies have masks of dark blue and sometimes a streak of blue on ears, along the back or on the tail, but these markings fade when the dog reaches maturity.

Height: dogs 14 in (36 cm); bitches 12½ in (32 cm).
Weight: dogs 35 lb (15.9 kg); bitches 33 lb (15 kg).

Irish Terrier

The red Irish Terrier originated in the districts around Ballymena and County Cork in South-Eastern Ireland. Of similar parentage to the Kerry and Soft-Coated Wheaten, with perhaps some old-type black-and-tan terrier blood, like them it would rather have a fight than miss one. It makes a good all-purpose dog and, like the Kerry Blue, can be trained as a retriever as well

Ch Lady Dinah of Montelle, by Ch Adamton Sergeant Major of Montelle, ex Merrydais Poachers Lady, br Mr Andrews, pr Miss A. Bradley

as a hunter of badger and otter. It also makes a good guard dog of handy size.

Its colour indicates that it is closer in origin to the Soft-Coated Wheaten than to the Kerry, and as near as either to the Glen of Imaal. Good with children, it is an excellent companion for young and old and a fine protector of person and property. Despite a reputedly fiery spirit, which has cost it some favour, it is in fact easily trained and even-tempered when unprovoked. It was used for bolting foxes and killing vermin and rabbits. Its recklessness in a fight has earned it the name of 'daredevil'. Always sure of itself, it can at times be rather independent and requires an energetic owner to keep it in hand.

Its jaunty showmanship and smart racy appearance in the ring always catch the eye. First shown in Dublin in 1874, and in Lisburn in 1875, it was separately classified in Great Britain in 1876. The Irish Terrier Club was formed in 1879 and drew up an official breed standard which has hardly changed over the years. It has a much racier appearance than the Airedale and steps out in the ring like a thoroughbred horse. In the same way as the Kerry, it will retrieve on land and from water and it has even been used to hunt big game in Africa; it was trained to act as a messenger dog in World War 1. Although the whole-coloured coat we see today is solid red of all shades, this was not so in the early days, when black-and-tans, blacks, greys and brindles were to be found; the latter colours were gradually bred out, leaving the distinctive reddish coloration. The Irish Terrier is very affectionate and thoroughly devoted to the master and family it loves and whom it will fight to protect, if required, with the courage of a lion.

The entire frame of the Irish Terrier is built on racing lines, combining grace and speed. The head is long with a flat skull which is rather narrow between the ears and narrowing towards the eyes; it is free from wrinkles and the stop is hardly visible, except in profile. The jaw is strong and muscular and of good punishing length, but not too full in the cheek. The foreface is well made up, delicately chiselled and devoid of wedginess. The hair is crisp and only sufficiently long to give an appearance of additional strength to the foreface. Lips are well fitting and nearly black. The nose is black. The eyes are dark, small and fiery. The ears are V-shaped, small and fairly thick, set well on the head and dropping forward close to the cheek. The top of the ear-fold is well above skull level. The ear is free of fringe and the hair on it is shorter and of a darker shade than the body. The bite is scissor, with upper incisors slightly overlapping lower, and the teeth are strong and even. The neck is fairly long, widening towards the shoulders and free of throatiness. A slight frill at each side of the neck runs nearly to the corner of the ear.

Forequarters have fine long shoulders sloping into the back. The legs are fairly long, perfectly straight, muscular and well boned. The elbows work freely clear of the sides; pasterns are short and straight. The chest is deep and muscular, and the body moderately long with a strong, straight back. The loin is slightly arched and the ribs are fairly sprung, more deep than round.

Hindquarters are strong with powerful thighs, hocks near the ground and stifles moderately bent. The hindlegs and forelegs move straight forward and hair on them is dense and crisp.

Feet are strong and fairly round, small with arched toes and black nails. The tail is docked to three-quarters, set on high, carried gaily and covered with rough hair.

The top coat is hard and wiry but must not hide body outline, particularly in the hindquarters. The undercoat is fine and soft. The colour is whole-coloured, red, wheaten-red or yellow-red. A white spot on the chest is permissible but is not liked on the feet.

Height: dogs 18 in (46 cm); bitches 17 in (43 cm).
Weight: dogs 27 lb (12.2 kg); bitches 25 lb (11.4 kg).

Kerry Blue Terrier

Coming from the rugged, mountainous County Kerry in South-Western Ireland, the Kerry Blue shares some of the mystique of those parts and the stories of its origins are often contradictory. Did it precede or follow its red-coated cousins, the Irish Terrier and the Soft-Coated Wheaten Terrier? What is certain is that the red terrier preceded it in the popularity stakes, being recognised in 1874, whereas the Kerry, although the Irishman's favourite and pure-bred from the first quarter of the nineteenth century and known as the Irish Blue Terrier, was not recognised until 1922 by the Kennel Club when it was first shown at Crufts. The Kerry Blue Terrier Club of Great Britain was formed in the same year and an American Club 4 years later. The breed received the ultimate accolade in February 1979 when Int. Ch. Callaghan of Leander took the Crufts Supreme Championship. Callaghan is a fine example of the excellent specimens bred consistently in the United States in recent years.

The Kerry had been bred from bluish, soft-coated types crossed with a mixture of terrier blood, including the Bedlington, the Glen of Imaal blues and perhaps even small grey Irish Wolfhounds. It was used to hunt badgers, foxes, otters and rabbits, and the Irish Club has always stressed the importance of its sporting qualities. Like the red and Soft-Coated Wheatens, it did not go to ground, but waited for the quarry to be bolted by ferrets or short-legged terriers. Its longish legs ensured success in pursuit. Like the Airedale, its multi-purpose rôle was developed and it was often used as a drover, gun dog and, of course, fighter and, in World War 2, it saw service with the Army as guard and patrol dog.

It does very well today in obedience tests and is as much at home in the water as on land. Its single non-shedding coat makes it a favourite indoors. Puppies are always born black; any tan or white markings should have disappeared by the age of 18 months, the blue or blue-grey shade often not developing until after that age. Although occasionally of uncertain temperament and wary of other dogs, it makes an excellent companion and house dog. It is long-lived, tough and extremely hardy. Its strikingly showy and outstandingly graceful appearance in the ring gives it the stamp of a winner and has earned it great popularity throughout Europe and in Canada and the United States.

Like all the Irish terriers, the Kerry Blue is one of the gamest in the field. It is a well-built powerhouse of a dog, always ready for action, alert and keen to perform anything it is called upon to do.

The head is long and lean in appearance, with a flat skull and slight stop, and the nose is jet black. The eyes are smallish, dark and full of fire. The V-shaped ears are fairly small and carried forward but not too high. The jaws are strong and powerful with level teeth, the upper incisors just closing over the lower; the roof of the mouth, the gums and lips are dark. The neck is strong and reachy.

Forequarters have sloping flat shoulders with elbows being carried close to the body. The forelegs are straight and well boned. The chest is deep, of

Fintona Bluehill Topaz of Jodasyl, by Louisburgh Tipperary Timothy, ex Ch Rathmorrel Princess, br Mr J. McGovern, pr Mrs S. Preece

moderate width, and the well-developed and muscular body is short-coupled, with well-sprung ribs, deep brisket, and of fine proportions. The topline is perfectly level.

Hindquarters are large and muscular with well-bent stifle and hocks close to the ground, allowing an easy, free rear action. The feet are round and small with black toe nails. The tail is set high and carried erect over the straight back.

The coat, like that of the Soft-Coated Wheaten, is silky, soft, wavy and abundant. The colour of the mature dog is a distinctive feature — any shade of blue with or without black points. A small white patch on the chest is permissible.

Height:: dogs 19 in (48 cm); bitches 17 in (43 cm).
Weight: dogs 37 lb (16.8 kg); bitches 33 lb (15 kg).

Lakeland Terrier

The Lake District of Cumberland and Westmorland has given its name to a breed of terrier evolved from the black-and-tan working terriers of local packs in the Patterdale area; it was in fact called the Patterdale Terrier at first and has also been known as the Fell Terrier, the Cumberland Terrier and the Westmorland Terrier. The Lakeland was bred by the huntsmen of these parts, such as the legendary John Peel, to cover the Fells and terrain like the rocky hillsides of the Border Country where the Border Terrier has always held sway. These hunts are horseless and huntsmen, followers, hounds and terriers all need great stamina and good feet in the chase of the racy grey fox among the screes and rocks of the fells. A similar specification was therefore laid down for the Lakeland as for the Border: not too short in the leg so that it could jump up on the rocks, but slender enough to allow it to follow the quarry down through the crevices, crawl after it, and have the courage and strength of bite to bolt or kill a cornered fox or badger.

The old-type Bedlington had been used to increase the gameness of these terriers and the topknot which still shows up from time to time in litters is living proof of Bedlington blood in the make-up of the Lakeland. To smarten its appearance, some Welsh Terrier blood was brought in and a touch of Wire-Haired Fox Terrier, from which the occasional white marks on feet and chest are derived.

A breed club was formed in 1912, but it was not until 1921 that the Lakeland Terrier was given recognition officially by the Kennel Club and first shown at the 1928 show. In 1931, Challenge Certificates were on offer for the first time and the type we see today was practically fixed, although the range of colours is not so wide now as it was in those days; preference now is towards bi-colours or whole-colours, solid black being well liked in Scandinavia.

The Lakeland has proved itself to be an excellent show dog and a favourite of the professional handler as its coat needs similar careful preparation and stripping to that of the Wire Fox Terrier and, when well presented, it takes a lot of beating. The breed is getting very popular in the United States, Ch. Stingray of Deryabah being the only dog to win Best in Show at both Crufts and Westminster (New York) shows. It is very smart in appearance and, when required, as hard a worker as any. Its sound calm temperament, general alertness and moderate size make it an ideal family dog and guard, suitable for both town and country.

The well-balanced head is that of a workmanlike dog. The skull is flat and refined. Foreface and jaws are powerful and the muzzle is broad and not too long. The length of the head from the stop to the tip of the nose should not exceed that from the occiput to the stop. The cheeks are flat-sided. The nose is black except in the liver-coloured dog, whose nose also is liver-coloured. Eyes are dark brown or hazel. Ears are moderately small and V-shaped. They are carried alertly and placed neither too high nor too low on the head. The teeth are even, with scissor bite, the top teeth fitting closely over the lower. The neck is moderately long, slightly arched and free from throatiness.

Ch Copper Coin of Kama, by Ch Kenelm Tinker, ex Happy Wanderer, br Mrs C. Bentley, pr Mrs J. Rabin

Forequarters have well-laid-back shoulders and straight well-boned legs. The chest is fairly narrow and the back strong and moderately short.

Hindquarters are strong and well muscled with long powerful thighs, well-turned stifles and hocks low to ground and straight.

The feet are small, compact, round and well padded. The tail is well set on, carried gaily but does not curl over the back. The coat is dense and weather-resistant, with harsh topcoat and good undercoat. The colours are black-and-tan, blue-and-tan, red, wheaten, red grizzle, liver, blue or black. The liver colour is not seen so often these days. Mahogany or deep tan is not typical. Small tips of white on feet or chest are permissible.

The movement of the Lakeland is similar to that of the Airedale and Fox Terriers, that is, with legs carried straight forward, the forelegs perpendicular and parallel to the sides and the propulsive power coming from the hindlegs with a strong forward thrust.

Height: dogs 14½ in (37 cm) ideally; bitches 13 in (33 cm).
Weight: dogs 17 lb (7.7 kg); bitches 15 lb (6.8 kg).

Manchester Terrier

The Manchester Terrier descends from the old-type, broken-coated black-and-tan terrier of the Northern Counties and, to a small extent, from the Old English White Terrier. It was used largely for ratting in the early nineteenth century and, later, some Whippet blood was added to increase its speed for rabbit-coursing. Like its ancestors, it won its spurs in the rat-pits which were at that time associated with the public houses of the Midlands; a dog called Billy is reported to have held the record for rat-killing — one hundred, no less, in the amazing time of 6 minutes 13 seconds!

The ratting and rabbiting, smooth black-and-tan became very popular among the working classes in the Manchester region and throughout the Midlands generally. John Hulme of Crumpsall is said to have been one of the first to breed it seriously. At that time, its ears were cropped as it was considered more humane to have the ears cut off short in order to prevent their possible mutilation in action. When cropping was banned in 1895, it began to lose popularity, as the heavy ears with which nature had endowed it detracted from its former elegant general appearance. This fault has now been bred out and the present-day Manchester has V-shaped smallish ears which have given it back the smart alert look it had formerly. At the turn of the century, it was already appearing in dog shows and some exports were made to Canada and the United States where it quickly made an impact in the show ring, no cropping difficulties being encountered there as it was not illegal. An American breed club was formed in 1923.

The simplicity of the origins of the Manchester Terrier are in total contrast to the complexities of the coat markings, which are of great beauty and clearly defined. However, the very exacting colour standard as described below has, like the problem of cropping, proved to be something of a deterrent to many breeders and prevented it from becoming a popular dog, too much stress having been put on markings at the expense at times of soundness. In today's show dog, however, these drawbacks have been overcome and we now have a very smart and lithe terrier with a beautiful gleaming coat of classical coloration which has been reflected in the Dobermann, among whose progenitors it figures. It is also closely linked to the modern English Toy Terrier (Black-and-Tan), known in America as the Manchester Terrier (Toy), a miniature version of the Manchester obtained by crossing small examples of the breed with Italian Greyhounds.

The Manchester Terrier is an excellent watch dog, compact and clean-footed, and its short coat, which fits it closely, is clearly an advantage indoors. As a member of the family, it is much appreciated, as its affection for children is well known.

Keyline Mercenary, by Ch Prioryhill Baronet, ex Keyline War Bonnet, br Mrs S. de Forest Keys, prs Mr & Mrs S. B. Henderson

The head is long with a narrow skull, level and wedge-shaped. The cheek muscles do not show and the foreface is well filled up under the eyes, with tapering tight-lipped jaws. The oblong eyes are small, dark and well set in. Ears are small and V-shaped, carried well above the top of the head, and hanging close to the head above the eyes. The mouth is level. The neck is fairly long, tapering from shoulder to head and without throatiness.

Forequarters have sloping shoulders and a narrow deep chest. The forelegs are straight, set on well under, and of proportionate length to the body, which is short, slightly roached and well cut up behind the well-sprung ribs.

Hindquarters have strong legs which are parallel and well bent at the stifle.

The feet are small, semi-hare-footed with well-arched toes. The tail is undocked, short and set on where the arch of the back ends, thick at the joint and tapering to the tip, being carried not higher than back level. The coat is close and smooth, short and glossy and of firm texture.

The colour is jet black and rich mahogany. The muzzle is tan to the nose; the nasal bone and nose are black. There is a small tan spot (kiss mark) on each cheek and above each eye; the under-jaw and throat have a distinct tan V. The legs from the knee down are tan, except for the toes, which are black-pencilled, and there is a black thumbmark just above the feet. The hindlegs are tanned inside but divided with black at the stifle joint. Under the tail is tan, and so is the vent but no more than can be covered by the tail. There is a slight tan mark on each side of the chest. The colours must be clearly defined, not blending into each other.

Height: dogs 16 in (41 cm); bitches 15 in (38 cm).
Weight: dogs 17 lb (7.7 kg); bitches 15 lb (6.8 kg).

95

Norfolk and Norwich Terriers

The Norfolk and Norwich Terriers are amongst the smallest of terriers and are identical except that the Norfolk has drop-ears and the Norwich has prick-ears. In the late nineteenth century, the two types were bred and shown together as one breed and were recognised as such by the Kennel Club in 1932, but it was not until 1965 that they were separately classified and shown with great success at Crufts, when C.C.s were first offered to the Norfolk variety. They originated in the Norwich and Cambridge districts of Norfolk where they were bred by local sportsmen, like Fred Law, to hunt fox and badger. Rags, a little reddish terrier belonging to the Master of the Norwich Staghounds, Jodrell Hopkins, was the progenitor of the breed. Frank 'Roughrider' Jones, the Norwich whipper-in and terrier man, began breeding from Rags' offspring and, using various outcrosses, including the small terrier strain developed by Colonel Vaughan of Ballybrick in Southern Ireland from Irish Terriers, Glen of Imaals and Cairns, produced what became known as the Jones or Trumpington Terrier and later as the Cantab Terrier, a dead game little dog, which soon found favour with Cambridge University students and in hunting circles throughout East Anglia. Its short back and legs and general compactness gave it the advantage of superb manoeuvrability underground and made it ideal for its work. If one looks for differences between the two varieties, apart from ear carriage, the Norfolk is perhaps a shade more docile than the Norwich and has a slightly shorter coat. They are game without being aggressive and need only the minimum of preparation for the show ring. Of excellent even temperament and very affectionate, always ready for a game, they make ideal children's companions; at the same time their fearlessness and strong protective instincts make them fine watch dogs for home and property, and their particularly acute hearing renders them eminently suitable for training as warning dogs for the deaf.

The general appearance is that of a compact, low-to-ground, short-backed and showy little dog, strong and with plenty of substance about it. Honourable scars from working should not be penalised in the show ring.

The skull is slightly rounded, with good width, and the muzzle is strong and wedge-shaped, about one-third shorter than from the occiput to the well-defined stop. The eyes are small, oval, deep-set and dark, with a keen expression. The ears are of medium size and V-shaped in both varieties, slightly rounded at the tip and dropping forward close to the cheek in the case of the Norfolk, erect when roused and with pointed tips in that of the Norwich. The jaws and teeth are strong with scissor bite and tight lips. The neck is muscular and not too short on well-laid-back shoulders.

Forequarters are powerful with elbows close in, short straight legs and

Ch Trundell Barnstormer, by Ch Squirreldene Barnaby, ex Bluecedars Honey Bell, br/pr Mrs V. Waters (Norwich)

pasterns firm and upright. The legs move straight forward. The body is compact with short back from withers to root of tail, good depth and level topline. Ribs are well sprung with short loin.

Hindquarters are broad and muscular with well-turned stifle; the hocks are well let down and parallel viewed from the rear, and have great powers of propulsion. Hindlegs follow in the track of forelegs when moving, and showing the pads.

The feet are round, cat-like and well padded, pointing straight forward. The tail is medium-docked, set on high and carried erect.

The coat is hard, wiry and straight, lying close to the body, and with a thick weatherproof undercoat, longer and rougher on neck and shoulders forming a ruff. Hair on head and ears is short and smooth. The colours are red, red-wheaten, black-and-tan or grizzle. White markings are undesirable but do not disqualify. Norfolk and Norwich Terriers should keep their heads and tails up in the ring without the assistance of the handler; there should be no 'topping and tailing'.

Height: dogs 10 in (25 cm); bitches 9 in (23 cm).
Weight: dogs 10 lb (4.5 kg); bitches 9 lb (4.1 kg).

Scottish Terrier

This breed was first shown as the Aberdeen Terrier, as they were most prolific in and around the city of granite, and later as the Scottish Terrier. A

Ch Stuane Highland Empress, by Ch Kennelgarth Edwin, ex Ch Stuane Princess Royale, br/pr Mr S. Plane

breed club was formed in 1882 and drew up a standard which has varied but little since. The American standard was drawn up in 1925 which allowed for a dog to be a little lighter in weight. Known as the Scottie for short, it is a great favourite at shows. It makes an excellent companion and watch dog, but tends to be somewhat standoffish with people it doesn't know and to become devoted to only one member of the family. Like all Scotland's group of terriers, it has been used against badgers and foxes, its strong compact body and muscular quarters making it especially effective underground. Ian Best of Aberdeen was the breeder to whom most credit must be given for the development by line-breeding of this dog towards the close of the nineteenth century, and it is largely he who gave it the distinctive, powerful silhouette and smart appearance we know so well today. If the Chow Chow has the sure-footedness of a cat, the Scottie has some feline characteristics also as far as behaviour is concerned, for instance the marked independence and condescension it shows even to its chosen master. That it is 'cock o' the north' no one is more sure than itself.

The Scottie is a devoted and sporting companion and a good houseguard, being distrustful of strangers. It needs careful trimming for shows where it regularly makes an impressive appearance in spite of its rather neutral coloration. Although black is the most popular colour now, this has not always been the case, brindles of various shades being preferred in the early days. It is known as a symbol of Scotland and has a world-wide following, due to some extent to the constant publicity it has received, whether in advertisements for whisky or in *Ric et Rac* strip cartoons. President Roosevelt's dog Fala was the most publicised terrier during World War 2, appearing with world leaders in many news pictures.

A point of interest is its movement, at the same time both dignified and amusing, as it makes its steady progress forward without much apparent effort; and the ability to adapt to any circumstances and any climate is another of its qualities, making it equally at home in the country or in town, so long as it gets plenty of exercise off the lead.

Multum in parvo — great power and activity in a small compass — are suggested by the general appearance of the Scottie. The head is long but in proportion to the size of the dog, the length of the skull enabling it to be fairly wide whilst seeming narrow. The skull is nearly flat and the cheek bones do not protrude. The stop is moderate and the nose large; in profile the line from the nose to the chin appears to slope backwards. Eyes are almond-shaped, dark brown, fairly wide apart and deep set under the eyebrows. Ears are neat, erect, pointed and of fine texture. The bite is scissor with large teeth, the upper incisors closely overlapping the lower. The neck is muscular and of moderate length.

Forequarters have long sloping shoulders, the brisket being well in front of the straight well-boned forelegs and pasterns. The chest is fairly broad and deep between the forelegs. The body has well-rounded ribs, flattening to the chest and carried well back. The back is straight, short and muscular, with level topline; the loin is muscular and deep, powerfully coupling the ribs to the hindquarters.

Hindquarters are very powerful and broad in relation to size. The thighs are deep and muscular and well bent at the stifle. Hindlegs are well boned with well-bent, strong hocks pointing straight forward.

Feet are well padded and of good size, with well-arched, close-knit toes. The tail is of moderate length, giving general balance to the dog; it is thick at the root and tapering to the tip, set on with an upright carriage or with a slight bend.

The coat is weather-resistant, the outercoat being harsh, dense and wiry over a short, dense, soft undercoat. The colour is black, wheaten or any shade of brindle.

Height: dogs 11 in (28 cm); bitches 10 in (25 cm).
Weight: dogs 21–23 lb (9.6–10.4 kg); bitches 18–21 lb (8.6–9.5 kg).

Sealyham Terrier

Captain John Owen Edwardes, the squire of Sealyham, a village on the River Seal, near Haverfordwest in Pembrokeshire, was the founder of this breed of short-legged white terriers in the mid-nineteenth century; he bred them specifically to use with his pack of Otterhounds. His strain, with bloodlines running back to a bitch called Duck, was the result of crossing predominantly white, broken-coated hunt terriers resembling Jack Russells with other similarly built dogs, such as the West Highland and the Dandie Dinmont, to produce a super game terrier to hunt otter, badger, fox and polecat. In order to accentuate gameness in his strain, Edwardes would in fact shoot any of his year-old terriers which failed to kill a polecat!

The Sealyham Terrier was shown for the first time at Haverfordwest in 1903 and a breed club was formed in 1908 by Fred Lewis, who continued the good work begun by Edwardes. The Kennel Club recognised the breed in 1911 and challenge certificates were first on offer the same year at the Great Joint Terrier Show. The first champion dog was St Brides Demon and the first champion bitch was Chawston Bess Bach.

After World War 2, Sir Jocelyn Lucas of Ilmer bred his own strain of Sealyhams which he used in a pack like Beagles along with his Lucas Terriers which resembled the old-type, lighter-weight Sealyhams of the previous century. In the 1920s and 1930s, the Sealyham became very popular, more as a show dog than as a worker as it had become by now too heavy for its original task and altogether more tractable and peaceloving. Although it requires considerable preparation for the show ring, as with the West Highland, and despite a tendency to be self-willed if not trained properly when young, the Sealyham makes an ideal companion; it is an efficient and fearless watch dog, sharing as it does the resonant bark of one of its ancestors, the Dandie Dinmont. Like the West Highland also, its popularity among American breeders has been maintained and imports there have had notable successes at the Westminster Show. A height of 10½ in (26.7 cm) is generally preferred in the United States.

The Sealyham is an alert, active and game terrier yet of a friendly disposition. It moves freely with a brisk and vigorous gait and plenty of drive, presenting a balanced picture of great substance in a small compass. The general outline is more oblong than square.

The skull is slightly domed and wide between the ears. Cheek bones are not prominent and the jaw is square, powerful and long. The nose is black. The dark eyes are deep set and oval, but not small. Unpigmented eye rims are permissible. The ears are of medium size, slightly rounded at the tip and carried at the side of the cheek. The teeth are level and strong, with the canine teeth fitting well into each other; the latter are long for the size of the dog. A scissor bite is preferred, with the upper incisors closely overlapping the lower and set square to the jaw, but a level bite is allowed. The neck is fairly long, thick and muscular, on well-laid shoulders.

Forequarters have short, strong forelegs which are as straight as is possible, consistent with the well-let-down broad chest between them. Point of shoulder should be in line with point of elbow, which is close to the side of

Ch Topstage Mr Bojangles, by Ch Fieldron Spectacle of Gunnygrace, ex Ch Topstage Mrs Peel, br/pr Mrs B. A. Postgate

the chest. The body is of medium length, level and flexible with well-sprung ribs.

Hindquarters are notably powerful in relation to the size of the dog. The thighs are deep and muscular with well-bent stifles. The hocks are strong, well bent and parallel to each other. The feet are round and cat-like, thickly padded, and pointing straight forward. The tail, carried gaily, is set in line with the back; quarters should not protrude beyond set of tail.

The topcoat is long, hard and wiry, with a weather-resistant undercoat. The colour is all white, or white with lemon, brown or badger-pied markings on head and ears. Much black and heavy ticking is undesirable.

Height: dogs 12 in (30 cm); bitches 10½ in (27 cm).
Weight: dogs 20 lb (9.1 kg); bitches 18 lb (8.2 kg).

Skye Terrier

Like the Cairn, the Skye Terrier hails from the Isle of Skye and the Western Isles of Scotland. It is one of the original Hebridean terriers dating back to the sixteenth century and it is described by Dr John Caius, court physician to Queen Elizabeth I and joint founder of Gonville and Caius College, Cambridge, in his book *Of English Dogges*, the first dog book published in English in 1570. Its profuse coat and powerful jaws afforded it great protection against the foxes and badgers it hunted in those times.

The story of Greyfriars Bobby is well known. Brought to the Scottish capital by his equally dour master, a shepherd, it is said that Bobby paid a daily call after the latter's death to the coffee house they had been accustomed to visit, and there, for 14 years, he would be given his usual titbit by the proprietor. The dog would then return to his master's grave where he slept overnight and where he himself was found dead eventually. An effigy was erected in his memory outside the churchyard. A Disney film is based on this story.

Drumfearn the Conjuror, by Kirkleyditch the Wizard of Drumfearn, ex Ch Kirkleyditch Border Queen, br Mr W. Legg, prs Mr & Mrs V. H. Thomas

The fidelity of the Skye Terrier is indeed legendary; it is a one-man dog and does not make friends easily. In the old days, its hunting abilities were second to none. Queen Victoria took to the breed in 1842 and posed with one for her portrait by Nicholson; this dog's name was Rona who thereafter became almost as famous as Bothy, the Jack Russell who recently went on the Transglobe expedition with Sir Ranulf Fiennes. Queen Victoria kept Skye Terriers for the rest of her life. This of course helped enormously to boost their popularity and they are to be seen in many of the beautiful scenes painted by Landseer.

The Skye has changed little since then, except that breeders have accentuated the length of the back — indeed the Skye is the only terrier for which the Kennel Club quotes an overall length from tip of nose to end of tail. They also developed the profuseness of the coat to make a very eye-catching show dog; all this has been done however at the expense of its working abilities. One advantage is that the coat requires no special preparation for showing. It makes an exclusive, sensitive, dignified and faithful friend, but don't be too familiar with one if it doesn't know you. Although it is definitely not vicious, it was not for nothing that the Skye Terrier Club of Scotland chose as its motto 'Wha dour meddle wi' me?'

The head is long and the jaws are powerful. The eyes are hazel, preferably dark, of medium size, close set and full of expression. Ears can be either prick or drop. Pricked ears are of medium size and gracefully feathered, erect at the outer edges and slanting towards each other at the inner edge from peak to skull. Dropped ears are larger and hang straight, lying flat and close at the front. The nose is black and the bite level. The neck is long and slightly crested.

Forequarters have broad shoulders close to the body and a deep chest. Legs are short and muscular. The body is long and low with a level back. Ribs are well sprung, giving a flattish appearance to the sides.

Hindquarters and flanks are well developed. Hindlegs are short and muscular and do not have dewclaws.

Feet are large and point forward. When the tail is hanging, the upper part is pendulous and the lower half is thrown back in a curve. When it is raised, it forms a prolongation of the back, neither rising higher nor curling up.

The coat is of great importance. It is double, having a short, close, soft and woolly undercoat and a long, hard, straight and flat overcoat which is free from crisp and curl. The hair on the head is shorter and softer, veiling the forehead and eyes. On the ears, the hair overhangs inside and falls down to mingle with the side locks, surrounding the ears, fringe-like and allowing their shape to appear. The tail is gracefully feathered. The colour is dark or light grey, fawn, cream with black points, or all black. In fact it can be any self colour allowing shading of the same colour and with a lighter undercoat, so long as the nose and ears are black. A small white spot on the chest is permissible.

Height: dogs 10 in (25 cm); bitches 9 in (23 cm).
Weight: dogs 25 lb (11.4 kg); bitches 23 lb (10.5 kg).
Total length: dogs 41½ in (105 cm); bitches 40 in (102 cm).

Soft-Coated Wheaten Terrier

A good-tempered dog, the Soft-Coated Wheaten Terrier has been bred in the South of Ireland for hundreds of years and is considered by many to be the original Irish terrier and the ancestor of the red Irish Terrier and the Kerry Blue. The story goes that a Wheaten bitch had been mated to a blue dog that had come ashore from a shipwreck in Tralee Bay some 200 years ago and that the blue puppies from this mating were the first of the Blues. The Wheaten was used as a terrier for sports such as otter-hunting and badger-digging and, at times, as a herder of sheep and cattle, and even as a retriever — in short, it is a real multi-purpose dog. It is also a very hardy dog, its long coat being practically weatherproof, and, although not so fiery in temperament as some other terriers, it makes a superb guard; rarely aggressive, it is an excellent and affectionate companion for children of all ages.

A Soft-Coated Wheaten Terrier breed club was formed in Ireland in 1934 and the dog was shown at the Dublin Championship show and recognised by the Irish Kennel Club in 1937. The English Kennel Club recognised it in 1943 and it appeared at Crufts the same year. The first champion of the breed rejoiced in the name of Ch. Charlie Tim, closely followed by Ch. Kingdom Leander, who also qualified at Field Trials. A Wheaten breed club was formed in the United States of America in 1962, but it was not until 1973 that the breed was recognised by the American Kennel Club, although a few good examples of the breed had been in that country since soon after World War 2. The Kennel Club of Canada gave its recognition in 1978 and the Wheaten is making great progress there now.

It is a natural dog of medium size, no trimming of its non-shedding coat being needed for the show ring. A game and truly Irish terrier, it is above all a tireless happy extrovert, always ready for fun with the family it adores; it is now quite rightly gaining in popularity in show circles, a striking figure as it stands compact and four-square in the ring in its beautiful wheaten coat which is its most distinctive feature. Puppies are born dark in colour and the final clear wheaten shade is not achieved until 18 or 24 months of age, when the texture of the coat has become stabilised. Of a very even temperament, it has recently proved its worth at obedience trials. Its intelligence is outstanding and it makes an excellent house dog. It is an active strong dog and requires plenty of exercise in open country. Wheaten exhibitors are becoming gradually more numerous, especially in the South of England, and the breed now is gaining many new friends in Scandinavia, West Germany and Switzerland.

The head is impressive and of moderate length, with the hair falling forward over the eyes and with a flat skull of moderate width. The stop is well defined and the cheek bones are not prominent. The distance from eye to nose tip is shorter than from eye to occiput. The muzzle is square and straight, its topline being parallel with the skull. The nose is black and fairly large. The eyes are of medium size, coloured dark hazel with black eye rims under strong brows, and the ears are V-shaped, folding at skull level, thin, smallish, fringed and lying close to the cheek. The jaws are strong and punishing, with large teeth and scissor bite, and the lips are tight and black. The neck is fairly long, strong and muscular, slightly arched and widening gradually to the shoulders.

Ch Finchwood Irish Mist, the first Champion of the breed in this country, by Binheath Winston of Finchwood, ex Binheath Mickle Miss, br/pr Mrs B. Burgess

Forequarters have long well-laid-back shoulders and the well-boned forelegs are dead straight, viewed from any angle, with strong springy pasterns. The chest is moderately wide and deep, and the body compact, close-coupled with powerful short loins and level back. The ribs are well sprung.

Hindquarters have strong and muscular thighs and well-developed hindlegs with well-bent stifles and hocks well let down and parallel.

Feet point straight forward and are strong and compact, well padded and have black toenails. The moderately thick tail is docked to 4 or 5 in (10 or 12.7 cm) and, set high, it is carried gaily, but not over the back.

The silky coat is of great beauty, being soft to the touch with loose waves or large light curls, falling naturally. The coat, which must not stand off, should be abundant and flowing all over the body, but especially on the head and legs, and it does not change in length or texture with the seasons. No trimming is necessary, apart from a little tidying up of the outline for show purposes. The final coloration of clear ripening wheat is not reached until maturity, when any darker shading will have disappeared.

A graceful, free and lively movement, with long low strides, straight action and head and tail held high, completes the picture of a fine elegant terrier.

Height: dogs 18–19½ in (46–49 cm); bitches 17–18 in (43–46 cm).
Weight: dogs 35–45 lb (15.9–20.4 kg); bitches 32–42 lb (14.5–19.1 kg).

Staffordshire Bull Terrier

Judging by recent show entries, the Stafford is one of the most popular terriers of today. Another of the Bull Terrier gladiators, the *canis pugnax* type exemplified, there is nothing it would rather do than square up to its like and fight to a finish. It is a hard dog, like the hard-living, hard-fighting Black Country men who bred it. Of the modern dogs, it is the nearest in conformation to the original bull-and-terrier, the fighting dog of the early nineteenth century. Used at first against bulls, and sometimes bears, it became, when baiting was forbidden in 1835, the fighting dog of the pits and, when this too was proscribed, it continued to take part in illicit matches up and down the country from Staffordshire to Dartmoor and the quarries of Bodmin Moor. Scouts would be posted in remote areas to look out for police and big money would change hands at the contests which ensued. Amongst the terriers used in crosses with the Bulldog were the English White Terrier and the old-type black-and-tan, both of which have left their mark on many of the terrier group. Various types and strains were bred in the Midlands until a standard was agreed and the present-day dog appeared. A breed club was formed in Cradley Heath and a standard drawn up, and the breed was recognised by the Kennel Club in 1935. Then, in 1948, when the standard was amended, the height was reduced from 15–18 in to 14–16 in. The Stafford's popularity is due in no small measure to its multi-purpose ability, its courage, stability, intelligence and tenacity. Its love of children and keenness to guard them are legendary. It is in this dog that the true terrier spirit burns brightest and, when roused, the uncanny blue Stafford is enough to strike a chill into the heart of any intruder. Notable exploits and contests of Staffies are legion in canine history and include, as well as the bear- and bull-baiting already mentioned, badger-digging and baiting; indeed, in 1957, a dog called Gentleman Jim of Inver, belonging to Mr S.W. Craik of Northern Ireland, killed a boar badger in 25 minutes on the Stormont near Belfast. As far as ratting is concerned, one of the old-type dogs owned by Jim Shaw is said to have dispatched over a thousand rats in an hour and a half! It is no surprise therefore that, as a deterrent and guard dog, it has few equals, and yet its conduct in the home is absolutely impeccable. It was not until 1974, that it was finally recognised by the American Kennel Club, this being due to the co-existence of a bigger dog of similar origin called the Staffordshire Terrier, and later the American Staffordshire Terrier, in that country.

The Stafford is of great strength for its size and, despite its formidable musculature, it is active and very agile. The head is most impressive with a short broad skull, pronounced cheek muscles, distinct stop, short foreface and black nose. The eyes are preferably dark but may bear some relation to

Ch Ginnels Black Tuskyanna, by Ch Black Tusker, ex Ginnels Madonnas Moon Maid, br Mr Jones, prs Mr & Mrs P. Shoulder

coat colour. They are round, of medium size and front facing. The ears are rose or half-pricked and of moderate size. The mouth is level, the incisors of the top jaw closely overlapping those of the bottom jaw, and the lips are tight. The neck is muscular, clean cut and shortish, gradually widening towards the shoulders.

Forequarters have straight well-boned legs set rather wide apart. There must be no looseness at the shoulders or weakness at the pasterns, from which the feet turn out slightly. The body is close-coupled with a level topline, wide front, deep brisket, well-sprung ribs (a so-called barrel of rib) and rather light in the loins.

Hindquarters are well muscled, hocks let down and stifles well bent. Legs are parallel when viewed from behind.

The feet are well padded, strong and of medium size. The tail should be low set, of medium length reaching to the hock joint, tapering to a point and carried low without much curl; a good whip of a tail.

The coat is smooth, short, glossy and lying close to the skin like that of a thoroughbred racehorse. The colours are red, fawn, brindle, black, blue or any of these colours with white. An all-white ground ticked with black is very showy. Black-and-tan or liver are not liked.

Height: dogs 15–16 in (38–41 cm); bitches 14–15 in (36–38 cm).
Weight: dogs 28–38 lb (12.7–17.2 kg); bitches 24–34 lb (10.9–15.4 kg).

Welsh Terrier

Dating back to the eighteenth century, the Welsh Terrier, one of the oldest of terrier breeds, comes, like the Sealyham, from Wales. Its progenitors were the old broken-coated black-and-tan terriers which have had such a great influence on many breeds of terrier. The huntsmen of Wales remained faithful to the black-and-tan coloration for their long-legged terriers when others elsewhere had begun to favour dominantly white dogs. The Irish Terrier and the Airedale played a part in its early development, and, later, the Lakeland was used to reduce the size and improve the outline.

The Jones family of Ynysfor had bred and used this type of working terrier from the middle of the eighteenth century to hunt fox, otter, badger and marten in the mountainous region of Merionethshire and Caernarvonshire. A hard-bitten game terrier, a good water dog and able to work with gun or ferret, it is still used by the hunts today, running alongside the hounds, but the show dogs we see in the ring are refined examples of the breed and, although less suited to working now, make excellent watch and house dogs and affectionate companions, loving plenty of exercise.

A breed club was formed and the first show was held at Pwllheli in 1885; the Kennel Club recognised the breed the following year. At the Llangollen show, of which Queen Victoria was patron in 1889, they were shown as Welsh Black-and-Tan Rough-Coated terriers. The Welsh Terrier was exported to America at the end of the nineteenth century and shown there first in 1898 and, in,1900, the Welsh Terrier Club of America was formed. There were classes for the breed at the Westminster Show in 1901. It has also been welcomed on the Continent, where its beauty and working ability have been especially appreciated. Its popularity has steadily increased in this century and, largely due to its strong constitution, handy size and suitability for town or country life, it has gained favour among connoisseurs throughout the world, the peak of popularity being reached after World War 2. Two fine specimens of the breed have become Supreme Champion at Crufts: Ch. Twinstar Dyma Fi in 1951 and Ch. Sandstorm Saracen in 1959. Its beautiful coat needs careful preparation for the show ring where it stands out in the terrier group like a beautiful piece of sculpture.

The Welsh terrier of today is far more elegant than its predecessors but retains the same excellent temperament, intelligence and courage, yet it is less volatile than some, and handlers appreciate its tractability and lack of pugnacity; it is however well able to defend itself when required.

The head is stronger and more masculine in appearance than that of the Fox Terrier, the skull being flat and wider between the ears. The jaw is powerful, clean cut, deeper and more punishing. The stop is moderate, the

108

Bizylizy Busybody, by Ch Gerallt Welsh Dragon, ex Fredas Mandr Sheba, br/pr Mr Lars Adeheimer

foreface of fair length from stop to the end of the nose, which is black. Eyes are small, dark and deep set, with the glint of keenness. The small ears are V-shaped, not too thin, set on fairly high and carried forward close to the cheek. The mouth is level with strong teeth. The neck is of medium length and thickness, slightly arched and sloping gracefully into the shoulders.

Forequarters have long sloping shoulders, well set back. The forelegs are straight and muscular, with ample bone and upright powerful pasterns. The chest is of good depth and moderate width. The back is short and the body well ribbed up. The loin is strong.

Hindquarters are forceful with muscular thighs of good length, and the hocks are well bent, well let down and of ample bone. The hindlegs are parallel to each other and carried straight through when in motion.

The feet are small, round and cat-like. The tail is well set on, but not carried too gaily.

The outercoat is wiry, hard, very close and abundant, with a soft, weather-resistant undercoat. A single coat is undesirable. The preferred colour is pure black-and-tan; black, grizzle and tan are permissible. There should be no black pencilling on the toes and no black below the hocks.

Height: dogs 14½−15½ in (37−39 cm); bitches 13½−14½ in (34−37 cm).
Weight: dogs 20−21 lb (9.1−9.5 kg); bitches 19−20 lb (8.6−9.1 kg).

109

West Highland White Terrier

Colonel E.D. Malcolm of Poltalloch in Argyllshire was the founder in the mid-nineteenth century of the strain of white Cairn-type terrier which developed into the West Highland White Terrier. Breeders of old-type Cairns were usually in the habit of culling any white puppies which happened to turn up in litters, but the Malcolms realised that the white dogs were more easily seen in the heather and rough terrain of the moorland. A local breed club was formed and produced dogs very similar to those we see today but closer-coupled than the Cairn, with broader skulls and slightly longer legs. They were known first as Poltalloch Terriers and later as Roseneath Terriers, after the Duke of Argyll's estate of that name. In 1899, a number of Roseneath Terriers were shown at Crystal Palace and, in 1904, they were first shown under the name of West Highland White Terriers at the Edinburgh show, with separate classification from the other Scottish terriers. In 1906, a breed club was formed in England and the standard drawn up. The breed was recognised by the Kennel Club in 1907, and the relative popularity of the West Highland took off from that time, both as show dog and companion. In temperament, it is a little more placid than some terriers and its coat does not need a lot of attention for general purposes. A ring full of Westies with their profuse snow-white coats is sure to catch the eye at the big shows. It is given special preparation for showing which really makes it a handler's dream dog, the ultimate in smart presentation with the hair on head and whiskers, and on underbelly and legs, carefully combed to give that perfectly immaculate appearance one knows so well and which has often earned it the title of Best in Show.

Yet, if put to it, it can hold its own in rocky terrain with any Lakeland or Border Terrier, being as tough as they come. Its love of children and domestic animals makes it an ideal small dog for all the family and its association with the black Scottie in whisky advertisements ensures that it is easily recognisable. Very hardy and active, it is a long-lived terrier of excellent temperament, sharing the cockiness of the Scottie, and is most attractive when seen freely stepping out beside its master or mistress. The West Highland is among the most popular dogs exported in recent years to the United States and the Continent where it has gained many top awards.

The head of the Westie is quite distinctive. The skull is slightly domed, presenting a smooth contour when gripped across the forehead. The distance from the occiput to the eyes is slightly greater than the length of the foreface. The head is thickly coated with hair and is carried high. The foreface gradually tapers from eye to muzzle. There is a distinct stop and a slight indentation between the eyes; below the eyes is well made up. The jaws are

110

Ashgate Rhum, by Ashgate Whaslikus, ex Ch Ashgate Glamis, brs/prs Mr & Mrs A. Thomson

strong and level; the nose is black, fairly large and forming a smooth contour with the muzzle. Eyes are set wide apart, of medium size and dark. They are slightly sunken under heavy brows, sharp and full of intelligence. Ears are small, pointed and erect, covered with short smooth hair, but without fringe. The bite is scissor, the upper incisors slightly overlapping the lower, but a level mouth is allowed. The neck is muscular, of medium length and widening to nicely sloping shoulders.

Forequarters have shoulders sloping backwards with broad blades lying close to the chest and with elbows well in, allowing the forelegs to move freely forwards. Forelegs are well boned, short, muscular, straight and thickly covered with short hard hair. The body is compact with level back and broad strong loins. The chest is deep and the ribs well arched in the upper half, presenting a flattish side appearance. The back ribs are of a considerable depth.

Hindquarters are strong, muscular and wide across the top, with short muscular hindlegs. Thighs are not too wide apart, the hocks well bent and well set in under the body, so as to be fairly close to each other.

Forefeet are larger than hindfeet, round, strong, thickly padded and covered with short hard hair. Hindfeet are also thickly padded. Pads and nails should be black. The tail is undocked, 5–6 in (12.7–15.23 cm) long, straight and covered with hard hair and carried jauntily.

The coat is pure white, the outercoat consisting of hard straight hair and the undercoat being soft, close and furry.

Height: dogs 11 in (28 cm); bitches 10 in (25 cm).
Weight: dogs 14 lb (6.4 kg); bitches 13 lb (5.9 kg).

111

Jack Russell Terrier

Numerically, the Jack Russell is the most popular terrier in Britain today, but, not yet recognised by the Kennel Club, it is unable to compete at shows other than those organised by the hunts and their supporters, which are held mostly in the summer. Young Jack Russell, when he was a student at Oxford University, had the good fortune in 1819 to buy from his local milkman a little terrier bitch which had taken his fancy. She was nearly all white with tan patches over the eyes and a tan dot on her back near the tail. She was broken-coated and had medium-length legs — just the dog he had been looking for to take home to Devon to pursue his favourite sports of fox- and hare-hunting and badger-digging. This dog, Trump, was the first of the Jack-Russell-type hunt terriers, and he mated her to a broken-coated black-and-tan dog.

Just as Cambridge University students were instrumental in the development of the Norfolk and Norwich terriers, the Jack Russell owes its existence to an undergraduate at Oxford. Parson Jack bred for good temperament and intelligence, qualities which he considered just as important as hardiness and gameness. One dog he bred, called Tip, would often leave the pack and head for the earth it knew the fox would make for, to bar its entry when it arrived!

The hunting reverend of Swimbridge also took an interest in showing and became a founder member of the Kennel Club in 1873 and judged Fox Terriers at its first show in the following year. A friend of the Royal Family, he sold a painting of Trump to the sporting Prince of Wales (Edward VII) and this now hangs in the tack room at Sandringham. More than a hundred years later, his own brand of Fox Terrier has still not been recognised by the Kennel Club as a distinct breed, but the keen band of enthusiasts who form the Jack Russell Terrier Club of Great Britain are working hard to put this to rights in the near future.

The most famous and farthest travelled Jack Russell, the only dog ever to visit both North and South Poles, is broken-coated Bothy, who accompanied Sir Ranulf Fiennes and his wife, Lady Virginia, on the Transglobe expedition to the Antarctic in 1980 and to the Arctic in 1981–1982. He *played* cricket and football with the Transglobe team at the South Pole and took part in the final celebrations at the North Pole! Most of all he loved having games with the penguins and scrambling up and sliding down the ice floes.

The Jack Russell Terrier Club has produced an interim breed standard specifying an alert, active, game terrier with a good even temperament, a well-built, well-proportioned, compact working terrier with an easy straight action.

The head is strong with a flat, moderately wide skull, narrowing to the

Ridley Redcap, winner of many awards at Club and Hunt Terrier Shows

eyes. The stop is medium and the muzzle length from nose to stop is shorter than the distance from stop to occiput. The nose and tight lips are black, the jaws powerful and cheeks muscular. The ears are small, V-shaped, fairly thick and carried forward close to the head. The eyes are almond-shaped, dark and expressive. The bite is scissor. The neck is muscular, of fair length and widening to the shoulders.

Forequarters have well-laid-back, sloping shoulders, cleanly cut at the withers. Forelegs are of medium length, strong, straight-boned and set not too wide. Elbows hang perpendicular to body and work free of the sides. The chest is fairly narrow and not too deep, and it should be possible to span it with two hands behind the shoulders. The back is strong, of moderate length and straight, with the loins slightly arched, and well ribbed up.

Hindquarters are strong and muscular, with good angulation and well-bent stifle, and the hocks are straight when viewed from behind.

The feet are round and cat-like, with hard pads and pointing straight forward. The strong tail is set rather high, carried gaily and about 4 in (10 cm) long, giving a firm hand-hold. The two types of coat are smooth and broken-coated, and the colour predominantly white with black, tan, brown or hound markings, and often with a small patch or dot at the root of the tail.

Two sizes are specified for show purposes:
Height: 9−12 in (23−30 cm); 12−14 in (30−36 cm).
Weight in accordance with height: 12−15 lb (5.5−6.8 kg).

Bibliography

This includes a selection of the most important books on the subject, both factual and pictorial, with items entered under name of author and showing title, place of publication, publisher and date(s) of edition(s) where known.

HISTORICAL AND GENERAL REFERENCES

Before 1900

Alfonso XI, king of Castile *El Libro de la Monteria* Madrid, c.1350

Bernes, Dame Julyans *The Boke* [sic] *of St. Albans* St. Albans: the author, 1486 (This is the spelling in the original edition; later reprints and editions have Berners, Juliana *The Book of St. Albans*)

Bewick, Thomas *A General History of Quadrupeds* Newcastle upon Tyne and London: Bewick, Robinson & Dilly, 1790, 1791, 1792, 1800, 1807, 1811, 1820 and 1824

Bingley, W. *Memoirs of British Quadrupeds* London: Darton & Harvey, 1809

Buffon, le comte de (George Louis Le Clerc) *Histoire des animaux quadrupèdes* Paris: Imprimeries Royale, 1775–1789

Butler, Charles *The Complete Dog Fancier's Companion* London: Darton, 1819

Caius, Dr Johannes [John] *De Canibus Britannicis* (in Latin) London: Guilelmum Seresium, 1570; subsequent editions by various publishers in 1685, 1729, 1731, 1752 and 1819. Also translated into English by Abraham Fleming under the title *Of English Dogges* London: Johnes, 1576, and Bradley, 1880. Reprinted in facsimile in Washington by Denlinger, 1947

Canteleu, le comte le Coulteux de *Manuel de vénerie française* Paris: the author, c.1880

Cox, Nicholas *The Gentleman's Recreation* London: the author, 1674 and 1686; Browne & Rolls, 1697. Also a reprint of Part I in London by Cresset, 1928

Dalziel, Hugh *British Dogs* London: Bazaar Office, 1879–1880, and Upcott Gill, 1888–1897

De Salis, H. *Dogs: a Manual for Amateurs* London: Longmans, Green, 1893

Edwards, Sydenham *Cynographia Britannica* London: the author, 1800

114

Egan, Pierce *Sporting Anecdotes* London: Sherwood, Neeley & Jones, 1820; Knight & Lacey, 1827

Fairfax, Thomas *The Complete Sportsman* London: Cooke, 1758, 1760, 1762 and 1795

Fouilloux, Jacques de *Traité de la vénerie* Paris: the author, c. 1550

Friedrich, O. *Élévage de nobles races canines* Prussia, Zahwa, 1886

Gray, D.J. Thomson *The Dogs of Scotland* Dundee, Mathew, 1891

Jesse, George Richard *Researches into the History of the British Dog* London: Hardwicke, 1866

Lawrence, John *The Sportsman's Repository* (with illustrations by John Scott) London: Sherwood, Neeley & Jones, 1820

Lindecrantz, Erik *Cynographia* The author, 1756

Linné, Carl von *Systema Naturae* c.1740

Markham, Gervase (pseud.) *Country Contentments* London: Jackson, 1615, and Hartson, 1631

Mason, Charles *Our Prize Dogs* New York: Forest and Stream, 1888

Meyrick, John *House Dogs and Sporting Dogs* London: Van Voorst, 1861

Needham, T.H. *The Complete Sportsman* London: Simpkin & Marshall, 1817

Pearce, Thomas (pseud. 'Idstone') *The Dog* London, Paris and New York: Cassell, Petter & Galpin, 1872 and subsequent reprints

Shaw, Vero *The Illustrated Book of the Dog* London and New York: Cassell, Petter & Galpin, 1881; Paris: Cassell, Petter & Galpin, 1890

Shirinsky-Shihmatoff, Prince Andrew *Album of Northern Dogs* 1896

Smith, Charles Hamilton *The Natural History of Dogs* Edinburgh: Lizars, 1839–1840

Taplin, William (pseud. 'Veteran Sportsman') *The Sportsman's Cabinet* London: Cundee, 1803–1804

Turberville, George *Noble art de la vénerie ou chasse à courre [The Noble Art of Venery or Hunting]* London: Barker, 1575, and Purfoot, 1611

Twici, William *Art de vénerie* (edited by Sir T. Phillips) Printed privately, 1840

Walsh, John Henry (pseud. 'Stonehenge', ed.) *The Dogs of the British Islands* (articles by several contributors, reprinted from *The Field*) London: Cox, 1867, 1872, 1878, 1882 and 1886

Walsh, John Henry (pseud. 'Stonehenge') *The Dog: its Varieties and Management* London and New York: Warne, 1874 and 1896; reprinted later as *The Dogs of Great Britain, America and Other Countries* New York: Orange Judd, 1919

Youatt, William *The Dog* London: Knight, 1845, and Longman, Brown, Green & Longman, 1852 and 1854; Philadelphia: Blanchard & Lea, 1857

After 1900

American Kennel Club (ed.) *The Complete Dog Book* New York: Halcyon House, 1935, and Garden City, 1945, 1956 and 1964

Ash, Edward C. *Dogs: their History and Development* London: Benn, 1927; Boston: Houghton Miffin, 1927

Barton, Frank Townend *The Kennel Encyclopaedia* London: Virtue, 1903, 1928, 1932, 1946, 1949 and 1951

Bathurst, Seymour Henry Earl *The Breeding of Foxhounds* London: Constable, 1926

Bengtson, Bo, Wintzell, Åke & Swedrup, Ivan *The Dogs of the World* (translated from the Swedish) Newton Abbot: David & Charles, 1983

Bokonyi, S. *A History of Domesticated Mammals* Academia Kiado, 1974

Boorer, Wendy *Dogs* London: Octopus, 1982

Browne, Anne Gondrexon-Ives *A Guide to the Dogs of the World* Paris, Lausanne and Brussels: Elsevier-Séquoia, 1973

Bruette, Dr William & Donnelly, Kerry V. *The Original Complete Dog Book* Neptune and Redhill: T.F.H., 1982

Bylandt, le comte de (Henri) *Les Races de chiens, les chiens, le gibier, ses ennemis* Postema & Van Raalte, 1904. Also as *Dogs of All Nations* London: Kegan Paul, 1905

Cabassu, J. & Cabassu, H. *Les Chiens* Paris, Hachette, 1939

Cartledge, Joe & Cartledge, Liz with Cavill, David & Cavill, Angela (eds) *The Dog Directory* Bracknell, 1980

Cavill, David *All About the Spitz Breeds* London: Pelham, 1978

Chalmers, Patrick R. *The History of Hunting* London: Seeley Service, 1936

Coffey, David *A Veterinary Surgeon's Guide to Dogs* Tadworth: Kaye & Ward, 1980

Cruft, Charles *Charles Cruft's Dog Book* London and New York: Foulsham, 1952

Dangerfield, Stanley & Howell, Elsworth S. (eds) *The International Encyclopaedia of Dogs* London: Rainbird, 1973, and Pelham, 1973

Davis, Henry P. (ed.) *The Modern Dog Encyclopedia* Harrisburg, Pennsylvania: Stackpole & Heck, 1949, 1956 and 1958

De Waziers, J.L. *Chiens d'aujourd'hui, de chasse, de défense et autres* Paris: Flammarion, 1967

Dechambre, Edmond *Les Chiens, origines, histoire, évolution* (3rd edition) Paris: P.U.F., 1971

Duchartre, P.L. *Dictionnaire de la chasse* Paris: Larousse, 1934

Edward, second duke of York *The Master of Game, being the First Book on Hunting Written in English* (first published in 1406, edited by William A. and F. Baillie Grohman) London: Ballantyne & Hanson, 1904, and Chatto & Windus, 1909

Elliot, R.P. *Dog Steps: Illustrated Gait at a Glance* New York: Howell, 1979

Epstein, Helmut *The Origin of the Domestic Animals of Africa* A.P.C., 1971

Fiennes, R. & Fiennes, A. *The Natural History of the Dog* London: Weidenfeld & Nicholson, 1968

Fitz-Barnard, L. *Fighting Sports* London: Odhams Press, 1921

Fox, M.W. *The Dog, its Domestication and Behaviour* Garland S.T.P.M. Press, 1978

Fox, Michael *The Wild Canids, their Systematics, Behavioural Ecology and Evolution* Wokingham: Van Nostrand Reinhold, 1975

Glover, Harry *Batsford's Book of Dogs* Newton Abbot: David & Charles, 1972

Glover, Harry (comp., ed.) *A Standard Guide to Pure-Bred Dogs* London: Macmillan, 1977

Glynn, Sir Richard *Champion Dogs of the World* London: Harrap, 1967

Gordon, John F. *Rare and Unusual Dog Breeds* Edinburgh: Bartholomew, 1950

Hackwood, Frederick W. *Old English Sports* London: T. Fisher Unwin, 1907

Hamilton, Ferelith (ed.) *The World Encyclopaedia of Dogs* Ashford: Dog World

Harmar, Hilary *Showing and Judging Dogs* London: Gifford, 1977

Hart, Ernest H. *Encyclopaedia of Dog Breeds* Redhill: T.F.H., 1970

Holmes, John *The Family Dog, its Choice and Training* London: Popular Dogs, 1957

Horner, Tom *Take Them Round, Please!* Newton Abbot: David & Charles, 1975

Hubbard, Clifford L.B. *Dogs in Britain* London: Macmillan, 1948

Hutchinson, Walter (ed.) *Hutchinson's Dog Encyclopaedia* London: Hutchinson, 1934–1935

Johnson, George & Ericson, Maria *Hounds of France* Hindhead: Spur Saiga, 1979

Kroese-Croll, H. Stenfert *Le Chien* Paris and Brussels: Elsevier-Séquoia, 1960

Lampson, Sonia M. *The Book of Dogs* London: Country Life, 1963

Lee, Rawdon B. *A History and Description of the Modern Dogs of Great Britain and Ireland — Sporting Division* (with illustrations by Arthur Wardle) London: Cox, 1906

Leighton, Robert *The Complete Book of the Dog* London and New York: Cassell, 1922, 1927, 1932 and 1952

Little, Clarence C. *The Inheritance of Coat Color in Dogs* Ithaca, New York: Cornell, 1957; London: Constable, 1957

Marvin, John T. *The Book of All Terriers* New York: Howell, 1964

Méry, Dr F. *Le Chien* Paris: Larousse, 1959

Oberthur, Dr Joseph *Gibiers de notre pays: histoire naturelle pour les chasseurs* Paris: the author, 1936–1937

117

Palmer, Joan *A Dog of Your Own* London: Salamander, 1965

Palmer, Joan *An Illustrated Guide to Dogs* London: Salamander, 1981

Plummer, D.B. *The Working Terrier* Woodbridge: Boydell, 1979

Portman-Graham, Capt. R. *The Practical Guide to Showing Dogs* London: Popular Dogs, 1956

Redlich, Anna *The Dogs of Ireland* Dundalk: Dundalgan Press, 1949

Ritchie, Carson I.A. *The British Dog: its History from Earliest Times* London: Robert Hale, 1981

Rousselet-Blanc, Dr Pierre *Le Chien* Paris: Larousse, 1955

Rousselet-Blanc, Dr Pierre & Rousselet-Blanc, Josette *L'Encyclopédie du chien* Paris: Denoël

Russell, J. *All About Gazehounds* London: Pelham, 1960

Schneider-Leyer, Dr Erich *Dogs of the World* (translated from the German *Die Hunde der Welt* by Dr E. Fitz Daglish) London: Popular Dogs, 1964

Sefton, Frances *Complete Dog Guide* Neptune and Redhill: T.F.H., 1970

Shaw, Vero *The Encyclopaedia of the Kennel* London: Routledge, 1913

Siméon, Y. *Chiens des villes et chiens des champs* Paris: Fabre, 1961

Smith, A. Croxton *Dogs since 1900* London: Dakers, 1950

Smith, Guy N. *Sporting and Working Dogs* Hindhead: Saiga, 1979

Stenton, Sir Frank (ed.) *The Bayeux Tapestry* Oxford: Phaidon Press, 1957

Sutton, Catherine G. *The Observer's Book of Dogs* London and New York: Warne, 1978

Sutton, Catherine G. *Dog Shows and Show Dogs* London: K. & R. Books, 1980

Sutton, Catherine G. *A Practical Guide to Breeding and Showing* London: Batsford, 1983

Swedrup, Ivan *Dogs of the World in Colour* (illustrated by Harald Wiberg) Stockholm, 1958; London: Blandford, 1961

Thomas, Joseph B. *Hounds and Hunting through the Ages* London: Derrydale Press, 1928, and Williams & Norgate, 1934

Tickner, John *Tickner's Terriers* Tetbury: Standfast Press, 1960

Tickner, John *To Hounds with John Tickner* London: Putnam, 1962

Troy, Suzanne *Dogs, Pets of Pedigree* London: Rigby, 1976

Turner, J. Sidney (ed.) *The Kennel Encyclopaedia* Sheffield: Encyclopaedic Press, 1907–1911; London: Long, 1907–1911

Vesey-Fitzgerald, Brian *The Dog Owner's Encyclopaedia* London: Pelham, 1965

Watson, James *The Dog Book* New York: Doubleday Page, 1905; London: Heinemann, 1906

HOUNDS

Afghan Hound
Brearley, Joan McDonald *The Book of the Afghan Hound* Jersey City and Redhill: T.F.H., 1978

Gie, Daphne *Afghan Hounds* Newton Abbot: David & Charles, 1978

Hall, William L. *The Afghan Hound* London: Gifford, 1971

Harrisson, Charles *The Afghan Hound* London: Popular Dogs, 1979

Kauffman, S.A. *The Afghan Hound* Washington: Denlinger

McCarthy, Dennis *The Afghan Hound* Edinburgh: Bartholomew, 1977

Miller, Constance O. & Gilbert, Edward M. *The Complete Afghan Hound* New York: Howell, 1965

Niblock, M. *The Book of the Afghan Hound* London: K. & R. Books, 1979

Pisano, Beverley *Afghan Hounds* Jersey City and Redhill: T.F.H., 1980

Sutton, Catherine G. *The Afghan Hound* Leicester: South Group, 1982

Basenji
Green, E.M. *The Basenji* Washington: Denlinger, 1970

Shafer, J. & Morley, B. *Raise and Train the Basenji* Jersey City and Redhill: T.F.H., 1972

Williams, Veronica Tudor *Basenjis, the Barkless Dogs* The author, 1946; Newton Abbot: David & Charles

Basset Hound
Appleton, Douglas H. *The Basset Hound Handbook* London: Nicholson & Watson, 1960

Braun, Mercedes *The Complete Basset Hound* New York: Howell, 1965, and later as *The New Complete Basset Hound*

Daglish, Eric Fitch *The Basset Hound Handbook* London: Foyle, 1965

Hart, Ernest H. *This is the Basset Hound* Jersey City and Redhill: T.F.H., 1979

Johnston, George *The Basset Hound* London: Popular Dogs, 1974

Rowett Johns, Jeanne *All About the Basset Hound* London: Pelham, 1973

Wells-Meacham, Joan *The Basset Hound* Edinburgh: Bartholomew, 1981

Beagle
Appleton, Douglas H. *The Beagle Handbook* London: Nicholson & Watson, 1959

Berndt, R.N. *The Beagle* Washington: Denlinger, 1961

Gordon, John F. *The Beagle Guide* Neptune and Redhill: T.F.H., 1975

Gray, Thelma *The Beagle* London: Popular Dogs, 1963, 1970 and 1975

Howell (ed.) *The New Complete Beagle* (by noted breeders) New York: Howell, 1978

Hewitt, William Lovell & Dupont, Richard J.M. *Beagling and Beagles in the U.S.* London: Faber & Faber, 1960

Priestley, Heather *All About the Beagle* London: Pelham, 1972

Sutton, Catherine G. *The Beagle* Edinburgh: Bartholomew, 1977

Whitney, George D. *This is the Beagle* Jersey City and Redhill: T.F.H., 1955

Bloodhound

Appleton, Douglas H. *The Bloodhound Handbook* London: Nicholson & Watson, 1960

Brey, Catherine F. & Reed, Lena F. *The Complete Bloodhound* New York: Howell, 1979

Harmar, Hilary *The Bloodhound Handbook* London: Foyle, 1975

Lowe, Brian *Hunting the Clean Boot* Poole: Blandford Press, 1981

Whitney, Leon F. *Bloodhounds and How to Train Them* New York: Orange Judd, 1947 and 1955

Borzoi

Chadwick, Winifred E. *The Borzoi Handbook* London: Nicholson & Watson, 1952

Gordon, John F. *The Borzoi* Edinburgh: Bartholomew, 1974

Groshams, L. *The Complete Borzoi* New York: Howell, 1970

McRae, Gail C. *How to Raise and Train a Borzoi* Jersey City and Redhill, T.F.H., 1964

Dachshunds

Adler, Leonore Loeb *This is the Dachshund* Jersey City and Redhill: T.F.H., 1966

Brunotte, Hans *The Dachshund Guide* Jersey City and Redhill: T.F.H., 1970

Cox, H.G. *The Dachshund* Washington: Denlinger, 1955

Daglish, Eric Fitch *The Dachshund* (9th edition, revised by Amyas Biss) London: Popular Dogs, 1979

Denlinger, Milo G. *The Complete Dachschund* Washington and Richmond: Denlinger, 1947 and 1954

Harrap, Elizabeth *The Dachshund* Edinburgh: Bartholomew, 1977

Meistrell, Lois *The New Complete Dachshund* New York: Howell, 1971

Raine, Katharine *All About the Dachshund* London: Pelham, 1980

Sanborn, Herbert C. *The Dachshund or Teckel* New York: Orange Judd, 1937, 1949 and 1955

Deerhound

Bell, E. Weston *The Scottish Deerhound* Edinburgh: Douglas, 1892

Benbow, Audrey M. *How to Raise and Train a Scottish Deerhound* Jersey City and Reigate: T.F.H., 1965

Cupples, George *Scotch Deerhounds and their Masters* Edinburgh and London: Blackwood, 1894

Hartley, A.N. *The Deerhound* Peterborough: the author, 1955

120

Elkhound

Crafts, Glenna Clark *How to Raise and Train a Norwegian Elkhound* Jersey City and Redhill: T.F.H., 1964

Franclose & Swanson *Norwegian Elkhounds* Washington: Denlinger, 1969

Ritson, Lady Kitty *see under* Finnish Spitz

Wallo, Olav O. & Thompson, William C. *The Complete Norwegian Elkhound* Middleburg: Denlinger, 1957

Finnish Spitz

Ritson, Lady Kitty *Elkhounds and Finsk Spets* Bradford and London: Whatmoughs, 1936

Foxhounds

Acton, C.R. *The Foxhound of the Future* Worcester and London: Baylis, 1953

Bradley, Cuthbert *The Foxhound of the Twentieth Century* London: Routledge, 1914

Moore, Daphne *Foxhounds* London: Batsford, 1981

Greyhound

Ash, Edward C. *The Book of the Greyhound* London: Hutchinson, 1933

Clarke, H. Edwards & Blanning, C. *The Greyhound* London: Popular Dogs, 1965 and 1979

Dalziel, Hugh *The Greyhound* (11th edition) London: Bazaar, Exchange & Mart, 1955

Genders, Roy *The Greyhound Handbook* London: Foyle, 1960

Regan, Ivy (ed.) *The Greyhound Owner's Encyclopaedia* London: Pelham, 1981

'The Rambler' (pseud., ed.) *The Complete Book of the Greyhound* Dublin: Parkside Press, 1945 and 1949

Walsh, John Henry (pseud. 'Stonehenge') *The Greyhound* London: Longman, Brown, Green & Longman, 1853, 1864 and 1875

Ibizan Hound

Brearley, Joan McDonald *Ibizan Hounds* Neptune and Redhill: T.F.H., 1980

Irish Wolfhound

Gardner, Phyllis *The Irish Wolfhound* Dundalk: Dundalgan Press, 1931

Gordon, John F. *The Irish Wolfhound* Edinburgh: Bartholomew, 1974

Hogan, Edmund *The History of the Irish Wolf Dog* Dublin: Sealy, Bryers & Walker and Gill & Son, 1897

Pisano, Beverley (ed.) *Irish Wolfhounds* Neptune and Reigate: T.F.H., 1981

Starbuck, Alma J. *The Complete Irish Wolfhound* New York: Howell, 1963

Sutton, Catherine G. *The Irish Wolfhound* London: K. & R. Books, 1978

Otterhound

Mouatt, Hugh R. *How to Raise and Train an Otterhound* Jersey City and Reigate: T.F.H., 1965

Pharaoh Hound

Sproule, Dr Brian J. *Pharaoh Hound Management* The author

Rhodesian Ridgeback

Hawley, Thomas C. *The Rhodesian Ridgeback: the Origin, History and Standard of the Breed* Johannesburg: the author, 1957

Lutman, Frank C. *How to Raise and Train a Rhodesian Ridgeback* Jersey City and Redhill: T.F.H., 1975

Saluki

Burch, Virginia M. *How to Raise and Train a Saluki* Jersey City and Reigate: T.F.H., 1965

Russell, Joanna *All About Gazehounds* London: Pelham, 1960

Watkins *The Saluki: Companion of Kings* Fenrose

Whippet

Daglish, Eric Fitch *Whippets* London: Foyle, 1964

Douglas-Todd, C.H. & Douglas-Todd, K. *The Whippet* London: Popular Dogs, 1961

Freeman, Lloyd *The Whippet* London: Upcott Gill, 1904; New York: Scribner, 1904; London: Bazaar, Exchange & Mart, 1912

Pegram, L. *The Complete Whippet* New York: Howell, 1970

Renwick, W. Lewis *The Whippet Handbook* London: Nicholson & Watson, 1957

Wilson, Pauline *Whippets: Rearing and Racing* London: Faber & Faber, 1962

Lurcher

Plummer, D.B. *The Complete Lurcher* Woodbridge: Boydell: 1979

Plummer, D.B. *Rogues and Running Dogs* Woodbridge: Boydell, 1982

Tottenham, Katharine *The Lurcher* London: Pelham, 1983

Walsh, E.G. *Lurchers and Longdogs* Cherington: Standfast Press, 1978

TERRIERS

Airedale Terrier

Baker, W.E. *The Airedale Terrier* New York: Field and Fancy, 1921

Bowen, Aylwin *Airedales* London: Williams & Norgate, 1950

Buckley, Holland *The Airedale Terrier* Manchester: Our Dogs, 1905, 1910, 1913 and 1927

Edwards, Gladys Brown *The New Complete Airedale Terrier* New York: Howell, 1980

Hayes, Irene E. *The Airedale Terrier* London: Foyle, 1960

Miller, Evelyn *How to Raise and Train an Airedale* Neptune and Redhill: T.F.H., 1978

Phillips, W.J. *The Modern Airedale* Kansas City: Buttles, 1921

Australian Terrier

Fox, Mrs Milton *How to Raise and Train an Australian Terrier* Jersey City and Reigate: T.F.H., 1965

Hamilton-Wilkes, Monty *The Australian Terrier* Sydney and London: Angus & Robertson, 1965

Bedlington Terrier

'Redmarshall' (pseud.) and others *The Bedlington Terrier* Cardiff: The Bedlington Terrier Association, 1932 and 1935

Border Terrier

Horn, Montagu H. *The Border Terrier* Hexham: Catherall, 1967

Jackson, Frank & Irving, W. Ronald *Border Terriers* London: Foyle, 1970

Johns, Rowland (ed.) *Our Friends the Lakeland and Border Terriers* London: Methuen, 1936

Roslin-Williams, Anne *The Border Terrier* London: Witherby, 1976

Bull Terrier

Adlam, Gladys M. *Forty Years of Bull Terriers* Bradford: Dog World, 1952

Briggs, L. Cabot *Bull Terriers* New York: Derrydale, 1940

Drewes, M. *The Bull Terrier* Middleburg: Denlinger, 1971

Eberhard, Ernest *The New Complete Bull Terrier* New York: Howell, 1972

Glyn, Richard H. *Bull Terriers* London and Oxford: Hall, 1936, 1937, 1942 and 1950

Gordon, John F. *The Bull Terrier Handbook* London: Nicholson & Watson, 1957

Hollender, V.C. (ed.) *Bull Terriers* London: Williams & Norgate, 1951

Horner, Tom *All About the Bull Terrier* London: Pelham, 1978

Montgomery, E.S. *The Bull Terrier* New York: Orange Judd, 1946

Oppenheimer, Raymond, H. *After Bar Sinister* Ashford: Dog World, 1969

Oppenheimer, Raymond H. *McGuffin and Co., a Bull Terrier History* Bradford: Dog World, 1964

Rosenblum, Edwin E. *How to Raise and Train a Bull Terrier, Standard and Miniature* Jersey City and Reigate: T.F.H., 1965

Cairn Terrier

Ash, Edward C. *The Cairn Terrier* London: Cassell, 1936

Beynon, J.W.H., Fisher, Alex & Wilson, Peggy *The Cairn Terrier* London: Popular Dogs, 1977

Caspersz, T.W.L. *The Cairn Terrier Handbook* London: Nicholson & Watson, 1957

Johns, Rowland (ed.) *Our Friend the Cairn* London: Methuen, 1933, 1946, 1950 and 1965

Jacobi, G.A. *The Cairn Terrier* Washington: Denlinger, 1970

McCormack, Erliss *How to Raise and Train a Cairn Terrier* Neptune and Redhill: T.F.H., 1965

Whitehead, Hector F. *Cairn Terriers* London: Foyle, 1959

Dandie Dinmont Terrier

Cook, Charles *The Dandie Dinmont Terrier* Edinburgh: Douglas, 1885

Gordon, John F. *The Dandie Dinmont Terrier* London: Nicholson & Watson, 1959, and Gifford, 1973

Kirby, Mrs William M. *How to Raise and Train a Dandie Dinmont* Jersey City and Reigate: T.F.H., 1964

Fox Terriers

Ackerman, Irving *The Complete Fox Terrier* New York: Orange Judd, 1938; London: Kegan Paul, 1938

Beak, Linda G. *Wire Fox Terriers* London: Foyle, 1970

Dalziel, Hugh *The Fox Terrier and All About It* London: Upcott Gill, 1899

Pardoe, J.H. *Fox Terriers* London: Benn, 1955

Silvernail, Evelyn L. *The New Complete Fox Terrier* New York: Howell, 1975

Williams, Elsie *The Fox Terrier, Wire and Smooth* London: Popular Dogs, 1980

Glen of Imaal Terrier

Cleary, Eithne *The Glen of Imaal Terrier* Lisburn: Irish Canine Press, 1983

Irish Terrier

Jones, Edna Howard *Irish Terriers* London: Foyle, 1959

Kidd, George *The Irish Terrier* Washington: Denlinger, 1954

Montgomery, E.S. *The Complete Irish Terrier* Middlewood: Denlinger, 1968

Kerry Blue Terrier

Clarke, Egerton *The Kerry Blue Terrier* London: Popular Dogs, 1928

Handy, Violet E. *The Modern Kerry Blue Terrier* Manchester: Our Dogs, 1933

Izant, Edith *The Kerry Blue Terrier* Fairfax: Denlinger, 1983

Montgomery, E.S. *The New Complete Kerry Blue Terrier* New York: Howell, 1965

Schweppe, Frederick *How to Raise and Train a Kerry Blue Terrier* Jersey City and Redhill: T.F.H., 1965

Lakeland Terrier
Kirk, Archie Paton *The Lakeland Terrier* Billericay: the author, 1964
Weiss, Seymour N. *How To Raise and Train a Lakeland Terrier* Jersey City and Reigate: T.F.H., 1966

Manchester Terrier
Cassels, K.A.H. *The Manchester Terrier* Manchester: British Manchester Terrier Club, 1960
Mack, Janet & Riser, Nancy *The Pet Manchester* Fond du Lac, Wisconsin: All-Pets, 1956

Norfolk and Norwich Terriers
Fournier, B.S. *How to Raise and Train Norfolk and Norwich Terriers* Jersey City and Reigate: T.F.H., 1965
Monckton, Sheila *The Norwich Terrier* Stafford: the author, 1960

Scottish Terrier
Bruette, William A. *The Scottish Terrier* New York: Watt, 1934
Caspersz, Dorothy S. *The Scottish Terrier Handbook* London: Nicholson & Watson, 1951
Ewing, Fayette C. *The Book of the Scottish Terrier* New York: Orange Judd, 1949
Kirk, T. Allen *This is the Scottish Terrier* Jersey City and Reigate: T.F.H., 1970
Marvin, John T. *The New Complete Scottish Terrier* New York: Howell, 1978

Sealyham Terrier
Chenuz, Frida J. *Sealyhams* London: Benn, 1956
Lucas, Capt. Jocelyn *The New Book of the Sealyham* London: Simpkin & Marshall, 1929
Marples, Theo *The Sealyham Terrier* Manchester: Our Dogs, 1926
Weiss, Seymour N. *How to Raise and Train a Sealyham Terrier* Jersey City and Redhill: T.F.H., 1965

Skye Terrier
Atkinson, Eleanor *Greyfriars Bobby* (with illustrations from the Disney film) London: Penguin, 1962
Brearley, Joan McDonald & Nicholas, Anna Katherine *This is the Skye Terrier* Jersey City and Reigate: T.F.H., 1975
Miles, Lady Marcia *The Skye Terrier* Whitchurch: the author, 1951
Montgomery, E.S. *The Complete Skye Terrier* New York: Howell, 1962
Weiss, Seymour, N. *How to Raise and Train a Skye Terrier* Jersey City and Redhill: T.F.H., 1965

Soft-Coated Wheaten Terrier

O'Connor, Margaret A. *How to Raise and Train a Soft-Coated Wheaten Terrier* Jersey City and Redhill: T.F.H., 1966

Staffordshire Bull Terrier

Beilby, H.N. *The Staffordshire Bull Terrier* London and Glasgow: Blackie, 1948

Gordon, John F. *The Staffordshire Bull Terrier Handbook* London: Nicholson & Watson, 1951

Gordon, John F. *Staffordshire Bull Terriers* London: Foyle, 1964

Gordon, John F. *The Staffordshire Bull Terrier Owner's Encyclopaedia* London: Pelham, 1977

Gordon, John F. *The Staffordshire Bull Terrier* (6th edition) London: Popular Dogs, 1983

Hollender, V.C. (ed.) *Staffordshire Bull Terriers* London: Williams & Norgate, 1952

Rosenblum, Edwin E. *How to Raise and Train a Staffordshire Terrier* Jersey City and Reigate: T.F.H., 1964

Welsh Terrier

Schneider, Earl *Know Your Welsh Terrier* London: Pet Library, 1968

Thomas, I. Morlaig *The Welsh Terrier Handbook* London: Nicholson & Watson, 1959

West Highland White Terrier

Dennis, D. Mary *The West Highland White Terrier* London: Popular Dogs, 1982

Hands, Barbara *The West Highland White Terrier* Edinburgh: Bartholomew, 1977

Marvin, John T. *The Complete West Highland White Terrier* New York: Howell, 1961 and 1965

Pacey, May *West Highland White Terriers* London: Foyle, 1963

Sherman, Mrs Florence *How to Raise and Train a West Highland White Terrier* Neptune and Redhill: T.F.H., 1982

Jack Russell Terrier

Harmar, Hilary *Jack Russell Terriers* London: Foyle, 1974

Huxham, Mona *All About the Jack Russell Terrier* London: Pelham, 1975

Plummer, David Brian *The Complete Jack Russell Terrier* Woodbridge: Boydell, 1980

Smith, Betty *The Jack Russell Terrier* London: Longacre Press, 1962

Tottenham, Katharine *The Jack Russell Terrier* Newton Abbot: David & Charles, 1982

Tottenham, Katharine *This is the Jack Russell Terrier* Neptune and Redhill: T.F.H., 1976

Index

Picture Credits

D. Dalton: pp. 15, 20, 29, 33, 35, 46, 84, 98; R. Delaney: pp. 31, 107;
F. Garwood: pp. 83, 97; M. Henrie: pp. 12, 23, 25, 28, 28, 37, 39, 41, 44, 48, 50,
55, 57, 60, 62, 65, 67, 70, 72, 73, 75, 77, 79, 88, 91, 93, 101, 102, 109, 113; High
Society Studios: p. 17; Infocus: p. 105; A. Roslin-Williams: pp. 53, 82, 95; Rudolph
Tauskey (Tauskey Collection/American Kennel Club): p. 42; L. Young: p. 111.